ACKNOWLEDGEM

WØØØ8603

The quote, "Some want to live within the sound of church or chapel bell. I want to run a rescue shop within a yard of hell", is by C.T. Studd. Copyright permission is obtained by Wholesome Words; 2012 www.WholesomeWords.org.

All Scripture verses are taken from The Living Bible published by Tyndale House Publishers, Carol Stream, Illinois, 60188 and is used with permission of Tyndale House Publishers, Inc. TLB is attached to each Scripture verse. '

The quote by John Ortberg in Chapter 1 is taken from the January 31, 2011 issue of Leadership Journal and is used with permission of the publisher.

The book cover is designed by incredible artist and my friend, Graci Evans of Happy Valley, Oregon.

Supportive information for the book has been provided by multiple periodicals, websites, books, copies of talks given by Lillian Phillips as well as her diary, letters from China by Malcolm and Lillian Phillips, and timelines of some events were provided by Dr. Richard Phillips. Kathy Fairley, Sharon Earl, and Don Fairley Sr. provided descriptive information about their lives in Congo. To all of these, I am grateful for your time and willingness to share your story. Any errors in recording the story are completely mine.

To Christy, my daughter who nagged long enough to make me sit down at my computer and begin to write the story of our family, you are responsible that this book saw the light of day. To Janis, my daughter-in-love who speaks computer-eze, thank you for formatting the interior and making my mistakes disappear.

DEDICATION

With more love than you can possibly know,
I dedicate this book to
Eli, Addie, Keenan, and Keely,
my grandchildren.

You will shine as brilliant lights in the world in your
own unique ways and continue the legacy of the
abnormal family into which you were born.

Grandma

CHAPTER 1

This is the chronicle of an abnormal family. It didn't start out that way, but that is the way it became. When it began to be abnormal is anyone's guess, but it's been abnormal for a long time. No one remembers when it first began to move in that direction but it happened sometime before I was born.

The true stories written here border on outrageous. They are taken from the letters, oral history, and reports of others who shared the experience with our family. The journal would never make it in the "History" or "Biography" section at the bookstore. Fiction or fantasy sections, maybe.

We have first-hand experience with the painful realities of prison camps, starvation, terror, children who were separated from parents for most of their growing up years, living under-ground, threats of death, repeated loss of all belongings, untreated serious illness, dead bodies floating in the river behind our house, fleeing from drug-crazed rebels in the jungle, living for days on a pig-skin raft on the Yellow River, hiding in caves at night. All of us have developed symptoms of Post Traumatic Growth.

One of the most frequently misquoted verses in the Bible is, "God will never give us more than we can bear." We are given more than we can handle all of the time, but we are never in a situation that God cannot handle.

In our abnormal family we have grown up planting our roots by relationships not location. Some, probably most of us, don't settle down easily. We can't. We are restless. We don't throw off our pasts although the threat is gone.

We have a special knowledge of the world that we have experienced. This is a gift and a curse.

We not only are abnormal. We FEEL abnormal. We have an expanded worldview, not just from seeing other parts of the world but also from living there. We know what it smells like and that is different from reading *National Geographic*.

We have grown up speaking multiple languages, Mandarin, Swahili, Marathi, tribal dialects in Vietnam to name a few. We are multicultural for life. Living outside of the Western world has changed us. We will always see life differently from "normal" people.

We are a family of missionaries. Within the past four generations we have worked in Mexico, Venezuela, Ivory Coast, Gabon, Congo, Kenya, India, China, Viet Nam, Uganda, New Zealand, Burkina Faso, Canary Islands, and more. We have married missionaries, which add more "family" connections to countries of service. Most of the young adults and college students in our family have served short-term assignments overseas. No surprise. It is in our blood. The most reliable indicator of becoming a career missionary is to have been a missionary-kid, but that statistic is about 20% and we met our quota a long time ago!

We have shared some of the same experiences but of course no two missionaries or MK's are alike, even ones in the same family. One thing is sure. We are an abnormal family. Who could argue? Not everything that has been a part of our story has been frightening or difficult. Some has been hysterical, full of adventure, fascinating, along with wonderful love stories. These stories need to be told, too.

"Cross-cultural enrichment" in our family includes eating some bizarre foods, including bugs, weeds, elephant meat, bird eyeballs, stewed moose nose, steamed bamboo rat, snake broth, braised bear paw, and monkey. "Ground goat" is a euphemism for dog meat. If you ask about favorite foods in our family, it's not likely to be hamburgers, but it won't be ground goat, either. Some of us have been big game hunters, not as a sport but because it was preferable to hunger.

How many countries have we lived in as an extended family? A lot. In normal families people go to the Chicago. We go to Congo.

Most of us have had unusual school settings, some in boarding schools, some in jungle settings, most in other countries. We have memorized the royalty of England because we were in British schools. We knew less about what was happening in American politics.

We all have close friends who are nationals in their own country. We have had diseases that civilized people avoid: TB, hepatitis, dysentery, cholera, malaria, small pox, diphtheria, whooping cough, and boils for starters.

The cost of discipleship for our grandparents and parents was high. John Ortberg wrote, "God isn't at work producing circumstances I want. He is at work in bad circumstances to produce the 'me' he wants."

Some of missionary life has left us with emotional limps, but perhaps God uses our limps more than our strengths? Faith is not genetically transmitted. We choose obedience to Christ whether we live at Chefoo or Colorado Springs. My Mother's life verse, 2 Samuel 24:24, "Neither will I offer unto the Lord of that which doeth cost me nothing." The heritage we have received came at a price.

We are an abnormal family. Our growing up years will never make it into a recommended guide for parenting. When it was good it was very, very good, and when it was bad it was horrid. This is a book of suffering, adventure, terror, excitement, resilience and, grief. Mostly it is a journal of knowing God.

Time does not heal all wounds. Some wounds get infected. Being children of "The Call" doesn't necessarily predict noble outcomes. Our experience on the mission field in itself didn't determine the outcome in our own lives. The same water that hardens an egg softens a carrot. We had models that endured hardship and taught us truth, but they were flawed, broken people who failed us at times. Missionaries and MK's don't always have permission to grieve in their mandate to be "brave soldiers".

For some of us it was our parents who signed up for life on the mission field and we went along for the sometimes bumpy ride. The statistics don't demonstrate that being born into a missionary family necessarily guarantees a personal commitment to Christ, or, even a life free of crime, but to the degree that we are willing to acknowledge, we have not spent any jail time. How and why did we spiritually and emotionally survive? Perhaps these stories will provide some answers.

"Thou hast given me the heritage of those that fear thy name." Psalm 61:5 TLB

"Let us run with patience the particular race that God has set before us. Keep your eyes on Jesus." Hebrews 12:1-2 TLB

CHAPTER 2

It had been a busy two weeks. I was in Nairobi, Kenya speaking to parent groups, student classes, chapel services as well as meeting 1:1 with stressed children. But now the work was done and I was off to a safari on the Maasai Mara in the Great Rift Valley. I'd stay in a luxury-tented camp equipped with a private indoor bathroom and shower. It was my kind of camping.

Each day we would take three trips out to search for the "Big Five," Cape buffalo, elephants, rhinos, lions, and leopards. We rode in the safety of an open top Jeep with the doors closed. Our African driver was friendly and confident. I was friendly. He drove us close to lions and when they looked annoyed, we got out of the way quickly.

On the first day we were provided a lecture about survival in this wild land. For one thing, if a hippo charges you it's wise to make an abrupt right turn because they don't navigate corners well. I thought this was a joke. Turns out I was the only one laughing. For another thing, the speaker said we should always completely zip up our tents each time we left since there were monstrous snakes who would slither in for a nap. He had my undivided attention on that one. My tent was a few feet away from a sharp decline. Below were 30 hippos that mostly basked in the sun by the river, but periodically looked up at me apparently deciding if there was too much fat on my body to be worth the uphill climb.

At the close of the final drive that day I returned to camp just as it was getting dark, had a wonderful dinner in the open air dining room shared by noisy monkeys, and then began the short walk to my tent. I was glad to have a flashlight.

The tent had been lighted by a kerosene lantern in the center of the tent, a thoughtful gesture by the camp staff. Good thing. It was totally dark at camp, no traffic lights, no streetlights, no night light in the bathroom. I wouldn't be able to see my hand in front of me once the lantern was out.

I brushed my teeth, pulled on my flannel nightgown and blew out the lamp. I reached over to my bed to throw back the covers and something moved! Not a small something either, it was wider than my hand, leathery, and definitely moving!

My heart nearly stopped. I fumbled for my flashlight on the bed stand, afraid that the creature might have encircled it by now. What I knew about death by anacondas was not a pretty picture; slow suffocation would be a hard way to go.

With my hands shaking I managed to find the flashlight and the matches nearby and get the lantern lit. I hoped I could get the tent unzipped and escape in time. I worked up my courage and turned toward my bed to discover that there in the center of my bed was the hot water bottle that the staff had placed for my comfort.

It was a tough decision but I decided not to share the "snake incident" with my Jeep companions the next morning. Not that they wouldn't have loved hearing it. I just wasn't up for the laughing.

Life on the Mara was not what I expected and neither is life on the mission field.

This is the story of our family. It is a tale about living as missionaries and the events that un-folded, which were not what we anticipated. Commitment to Christ means that HE writes the story. How the chapters unfold is His business. It requires trusting God with the fine print. The cost of discipleship in our family has included letting go of the fantasy of control and hanging on to Jesus when it is totally dark.

Most missionaries go to the field clearly focused on serving nationals, meeting health needs, creating alphabets so the Bible can be translated into that language, preaching and teaching, planting churches, and a host of other ministries. Although new missionaries recognize that there is potential danger and sacrifice in their chosen career, the risks may be minimized while the focus on following God "to the ends of the earth" is plainly in view. They trust God to take care of them. As one said, "Keeping me alive is God's business."

But life on the mission field can be extraordinarily hard, sacrifices are excruciating, illness and death occurs more frequently without near-by medical care and expectations of making a difference sometimes are delayed. Young married couples that have children after they arrive on the field are faced with challenges that surpass what they ever anticipated. It is during these times that spiritual gold is formed. No one in our family went to the mission field anticipating that they would be heroes, but in the suffering gold emerged and heroes were formed.

As you read their stories I hope you will know the very rich heritage that you share.

"It was because He loved your ancestors and chose to bless their descendants....."
Deuteronomy 4:37 TLB

"Never forget what you have seen God doing....May his miracles have a deep and permanent effect upon your lives."
Deuteronomy 4:9 TLB

CHAPTER 3

Below is the current list of international service during the past four generations, beginning with our parents, Malcolm and Lillian Phillips. The individuals and families listed are connected to Richard Phillips, Kathy Fairley, Dave Phillips, and Doris Sanford.

ST =   short term missions up to 2 years
Sch=   attended school in that country
NGO= service with non-governmental organization

Children are included in this list of family missionaries because they were always involved in the work of their parents. They just didn't receive a salary.

Malcolm and Lillian Phillips:	China
Richard and Lillian Phillips:	Vietnam, Burkina Faso
Kathy and Gordon Fairley:	Congo/Zaire, Switzerland (Sch)
Kathy Fairley:	China
Dave and Marilyn Phillips:	Uganda (ST)
Dave Phillips:	China
Doris Sanford:	China; Kenya (ST)
Gordon Fairley:	Central African Republic; Gabon; Congo
Don and Dorothy Fairley:	Gabon; Congo
May Phillips:	Venezuela
Addie Burch:	Mexico (ST)

Margaret Phillips:	Canary Islands; Venezuela
Shep and Sharon Earl:	Kenya (ST)
Sharon Earl:	Congo; France (ST)
Shep Earl:	Mexico (ST) Australia (Sch)
Ralph Wolfe:	Kenya (Sch)
Ralph and Sharon Wolfe:	Kenya (ST)
Don Fairley:	Congo
Don Fairley, Jr.:	Thailand (ST)
Darlene Fairley:	Congo
Melody Lawson:	Uganda (ST); Haiti (NGO)
Jeremy and Jamie Phillips:	Uganda (NGO)
Jeremy Phillips:	Nigeria (Sch); Scotland (Sch)
Tilman and Esther Amstutz:	India
Mike and Christy Burch:	New Zealand (ST)
Christy Burch:	Germany (Sch); Sweden (Sch)
Diane Fairley:	Philippines (ST); Taiwan (ST); Korea (ST)
Aleda Fairley:	Uganda (Sch); Rwanda (Sch); Mexico (ST)
Eli Burch:	Mexico (ST)
Jeanne Miller:	Vietnam, Ivory Coast; Burkina Faso, Malaysia

Brian Miller:	Guatemala (ST), Belize (ST), Ivory Coast (ST), Switzerland (ST)
Sarah Miller:	Mexico (ST), Ivory Coast (ST)
Nathaniel Miller:	Mexico (ST), Guatemala (ST)
Jason Miller:	Mexico (ST)
Nathan Phillips:	Zimbabwe (ST), Ghana (Sch), Switzerland
Brian and Donna Phillips:	Switzerland
Donna Skinner:	Ivory Coast
Andrea Phillips:	Switzerland; Germany (Sch)
Hannah Phillips:	Switzerland
John Phillips:	Vietnam, Burkina Faso, Ivory Coast, Malaysia, China
Renee Phillips:	China
Macaela Phillips:	China
Lillian Phillips:	China
Riley Phillips:	China
Harold Amstutz:	Ecuador (ST), India
Elda Amstutz:	India
Ryan and Karin Johnson:	China
John and Ruth Schebenius:	Zimbabwe, Botswana
Steve and Ann Copeland:	Senegal, Fiji,

	St. Kitts
Steve Copeland:	Ethiopia
Ann Copeland:	Zimbabwe
John and Carolyn Amstutz:	Ivory Coast
John Amstutz:	India
Kenneth and May Amstutz:	Chad, France
Brian Phillips:	Burkina Faso,
	Vietnam,
	Ivory Coast,
	Malaysia
Ruth DesJardins:	Burkina Faso,
	Vietnam,
	Ivory Coast
	Malaysia
Maxwell Phillips:	Mexico
Harry and Ellen Phillips:	Mexico
Renee Bowman:	Cote d'Ivoire
Tim Sanford:	Mexico (ST)
Janis Sanford:	Canada (Sch)
	Mexico (ST)
Rilla Amstutz:	Africa
Doug and Anya Holcomb:	Mexico (ST, Sch),
	Lebanon (Sch),
	Egypt (Sch, ST),
	Turkey (ST),
	Kenya (Sch)
	Uganda (ST),
	Tanzania (ST),
	Jordan (Sch)
Doug Holcomb:	Sudan
Zeek Earl:	Kenya (Sch)

Rachel Earl:	Mexico (ST)
Tim Lawson:	Mexico (ST)
Ron and Char Holcomb:	Kenya, Sudan
Dan and Erin Holcomb:	Kenya (ST), Uganda (ST), Tanzania (ST) Sudan (ST)
Phil and Rea Holcomb:	Ecuador
Ray and Arlene Wolfe:	Kenya
Rick Kincade:	Nepal
Lois Amstutz Johnson:	India
Annika Johnson:	China
Latie Lamott:	Korea
Sarah Schuette:	Korea
Hannah Schuette:	Korea
Jeremy Johnson:	Sierra Leone
Rachel Johnson:	Sierra Leone
Zachary Johnson:	Guatemala
Katy Fairley:	Korea (Sch)
Annika Bettenhausen:	China
Buddy and May Morris:	Singapore
Marguerite Watmough:	India
Bonnie Fairley:	France (ST); Gabon, Congo
Dottie Classen:	Gabon, Congo
Betty Seng:	Gabon, Congo
Jack and Ruth Buck:	Borneo, Indonesia
Peggy Buck:	Gabon, Congo

CHAPTER 4

In China, white is the color of death and red is the color of happiness. Red is also the color of blood.

Before Malcolm and Lillian and their young son, Richard sailed to China in 1931 they had heard stories about the brutal cost of discipleship for those already serving there. The news wasn't good. But hearing reports of other people's experience and facing the challenges themselves was not the same thing. They knew that just 32 years before 189 missionaries had been martyred 47 of them in the province next to their soon to be assigned station. The martyrs were buried in a mass grave.

The Boxer Rebellion ("The League of Righteous and Harmonious Fists") was in full force at that time. It sprang up to discredit and destroy foreign influence. Racial hatred of foreigners was high. Vindictive harassment, killings, and uninhibited lawlessness defined the movement.

Since the earth was square and China was a circle within it touching the four sides, those outside the circle were "barbarians". Lillian weighed 99 lbs. at the time she and Mac went to China, so she was a TINY barbarian, but a barbarian, nevertheless.

During the Boxer reign of terror members roamed the interior of China killing missionaries and burning down foreign-owned buildings. Mail delivery stopped and food was scarce. Innkeepers would not allow a foreigner to spend the night, and signs were posted naming specific missionaries and stating that they killed Chinese babies and cut out their eyes.

Thirty-two years later the welcome mat was nowhere in sight for Mac and Lillian in Gansu Province. At times the only crowds Mac could gather came to stare at the cute white boy with red hair. Definitely worth the trip but not what Mac and Lillian had come to China to do.

Seven times in five months Mac had to hide the family valuables under the floorboards or under the roof tiles. Mac was shot at once while he was on the roof.

The animosity against foreigners made sense considering the bad behavior of many of these outsiders. Opium had been brought to China from England and now eating opium was all but universal. Lillian said that presenting the Gospel to a group of women doped up with opium was a challenge because women were unable to understand what she was saying in their mental fog. That may be an under-statement. Millions of Chinese died as a result of opium use and practically everyone who was not Christian ingested opium in Gansu. When little babies cried or were sick, the fumes from an opium pipe were blown into their faces and they were soon asleep. Lillian said that her best work was with young married girls who were not yet addicted. Opium addicts frequently committed suicide. The Chinese had good reason to hate white people.

Foreigners, too, had prospected for coal, iron and petroleum, taking the resources that belonged to the Chinese people apparently relying on a typical two-year-olds philosophy, "What's yours is mine, and what's mine is mine".

Foreigners behaved as if they were superior to the Chinese. They employed Chinese as servants. That didn't go over well because the Chinese knew that THEY were the superior race.

Long droughts and famine had found the people ripe for lawlessness. "The wrath of the gods who were withholding rain had to be appeased." Every crop failure, flood or famine was blamed on the foreigners.

During those years just before Mac and Lillian arrived, missionaries in Gansu fled for their lives, but it was 1,000 miles to the coast where they would be safe. Those who attempted to escape slept in small filthy inns used by muleteers, not inns for travelers. At times water was provided for baths at these hostels but it was 2 pints for every 5 people. So much for soaking in a steamy tub of warm water.

Half of the missionaries in Gansu who had attempted to escape the Boxers had dysentery. Imagine traveling by donkey with diarrhea! The rest of the missionary evacuees had large boils, contagious eye diseases and infected scabies. Chinese authorities would hold perfume while interrogating missionaries due to the belief that foreigners were innately unclean, and some were.

Somewhere between one-half to two-thirds of the children of missionaries died while escaping from the northern interior provinces, including Gansu, where Mac and Lillian would soon arrive. Spears and threats terrorized the children who did NOT die from starvation or infection. By the time Mac and Lillian were settled in Gansu the death of a child of missionaries was still common, and often a family had two or more children die from disease. General population deaths were even higher. Wealthy families took extreme precautions to protect their children from the other Chinese and the germs they carried.

It took six weeks to cross the interior of China and make it to the coast. Some of the inns along the way consisted of one room in a cliff in the mountains. One mule train driver asked for medicine for one of his men. The missionary watched him give it to a lazy mule. Amazingly the mule started pulling harder.

The Boxers tore up railroad lines, cut wires and occupied roads from Gansu to the coast. Armed bandits desperate with hunger scoured the roads.

Children were beheaded as easily as adults. At times the killings were not quick. The breasts of women missionaries were cut off and hung on city walls.

Some adults and children traveled with gangrene alive with maggots. Carts were driven over missionaries in order to break their spines.

Back in the United States, Mac and Lil were recently married and students at Simpson Bible Institute when they first heard about the need for 200 missionaries who were willing to go to the interior of China and preach the Gospel to people who had never heard it….and, to people who might kill them for sharing it. 203 candidates responded to the China Inland Mission call, Mac and Lillian were among them.

The "benefit package" promised isolation, hardship, rejection, suffering, hunger and possibly death. The monthly salary would be "variable;" each missionary would receive an equal share of whatever came in. There would be no 401K. They said, "Yes."

By 1912 the Boxer revolution was over, but the damage was done in the minds of terrified Chinese. Then eight years later northwest China would experience a devastating famine in 1920 and between 30-40 million people starved to death.

By 1927, just four years before Mac and Lillian arrived, civil war broke out in northern China and foreigners were targets again. Chinese would throw rocks at foreigners' backs so missionaries stood against walls, which was safer but did not guarantee safety.

Malcolm and Lillian arrived in China after the Civil war. The year was 1932. Two years later John and Betty Stam, fellow missionaries, were beheaded by a band of soldiers who were on their way to Mac and Lillian in an attempt to kill them as well. This was 1934.

The assassins led the Stams to a hill, tied them with ropes and called for people to come and witness the execution. Two Christians pleaded for the lives of John and Betty and they were beheaded, too. Their 2-month-old baby girl was left for 30 hours until a Chinese evangelist found her and took her to safety 100 miles away. The telegram home read, "Remember that you gave John and Betty to God, not to China."

John and Betty were among the 203 who responded to the call for service in China along with Mac and Lillian. In November 1931 Betty had written:

"We follow His train
The Bright Morning Star,
He led o'er the seas
From countries afar.
He gently says, "Come"

He supplies all our needs,
So forward, two-hundred,
'Tis Jesus who leads."

"And God has reserved for his children the priceless gift of eternal life; it is kept in heaven for you, beyond the reach of change and decay."
I Peter 1:4 TLB

CHAPTER 5

Language school for Mac and Lillian was about more than learning to speak Mandarin words. They also needed to learn the tones of the Chinese language which was not that easy! Later on when Mac preached one of his first sermons he mistakenly invited listeners to accept "gravy" as lord of their lives. Turns out the word for gravy and God are the same, but a different tone changed the meaning. Of course Chinese people were too polite to laugh so he continued the call inviting people to submit their lives to following gravy.

At language school Mac and Lillian also needed to learn to read and write Chinese characters with a brush and to eat with chopsticks. Manners learned in the United States were abandoned and replaced with loud slurping so the cook knew you were enjoying your meal. It was polite to reach across the table with your chopsticks to get what you want. You should never bother your neighbor by asking him to pass something to you. He is busy eating so if you can't reach the food you better stand, stretch and take matters into your own hands or in this case, into your wobbly chopsticks.

The books for study, including the Chinese Bible were read down and up, not across. They were told that when we read our Bibles we shake our heads, no, no; but when Chinese read it they are nodding, yes, yes.

They studied with new missionaries from Australia, New Zealand, Germany, and England.

Three of the five couples had small children at the language school and they sometimes talked about where they might be assigned to work. They assumed it would be near the coast, but when the assignment came, they were told that they would be stationed in the northern interior of China, in Gansu Province. Since the China Inland Mission worked in the northern part of Gansu and the Christian and Missionary Alliance in the southern part of the province, it made sense considering Mac and Lillian's backgrounds. Some of the single men were also assigned to Gansu so they would travel together. It took six weeks as they traveled by train, truck, boat, and the last week by mule.

There were no working railroads in Gansu at the time that Mac and Lillian and Richard were traveling, and only one motor road.

The trip to their new station was not without incident. When they were on the train traveling through Honan Province the train engine caught fire. Since they were in the desert there was no water to put out the fire and the baggage cars also burned, except the one car that contained Mac and Lillian's belongings. While passengers waited for repairs they got off to walk around. Lillian stayed in her seat because one-year old Richard was taking his nap. While the passengers were gone a robber went through each car and robbed them, except of course the car where Lillian sat.

The end of the rail line was in Sian, a city notorious for hating Christian missionaries. The university there was controlled by communists. Prior to Mac and Lillian's arrival a school for missionary children had been located in Sian, but all of the children and their teachers had been murdered.

Mac and Lillian spent the night at the home of missionaries serving in Sian and Lillian and another missionary walked one of the dinner guests to her home. On the way back some college students came behind them singing loudly. Neither Lillian nor her companion understood the words to the songs. When they reached the house Lillian discovered that the back of her coat had been sprayed with acid and was completely destroyed. Her companion's clothing didn't fare any better.

Mac and Lillian had been in China for seven months and they had two encounters with communists. There would be more to come.

Going to China was both exhilarating and frightening. This was not a tour or a "short term mission trip." It was a lifetime commitment to a dangerous unknown.

For Lillian, the hardest part of leaving was saying goodbye to her closest friends. Beulah was one of the close ones. They wept and reminded each other that if they didn't meet again on this earth, they knew that they would be together in heaven and have eternity to talk. As a final gesture of her deep love for Lillian, Beulah promised to allow God to awaken her at any hour of the day or night during the years ahead when Mac or Lillian or little Richard were in need of prayer. She showed Lillian the prayer journal she had prepared. She promised to write the date, time of day and any special thoughts she had each time she felt a need to pray for them. Lillian also agreed that as much as possible she too would keep a written record of the specific times someone in the family was in need of prayer.

There were no phone calls, no e-mail, and not even regular mail with any consistency. The news about China that came to Beulah was mostly in the newspaper or on the radio, and that news was not good: there were communist, nationalists, as well as Japanese invasions and brutality in north China. American missionaries were killed; the school for missionary children was turned into a POW camp. It was definitely bad news.

Although Beulah did not hear directly from Lillian more than a few times a year, she knew that they must be in danger because she was losing a lot of sleep being awakened at night with an urgent desire to pray.

In China, Mac and Lillian were at times hiding in caves, traveling at night over steep mountain passes, going without medical care. They were hidden by Chinese Christians. On various scraps of paper Lillian jotted down dates, time, and the terrifying danger.

When furlough came, at a kitchen table in Albany, Oregon, the journals were laid side by side. Through tears and laughter, the two women compared notes. Dates, times, and events in northern China matched exactly with the silent alarm in a small town in Oregon that brought a friend to her knees.

"He knows every detail of what is happening."
Job 23:10 TLB

CHAPTER 6

Gansu was not a vacation destination. Not even close. It was poor and unattractive. In the winter when it was not covered with snow, the Province was one monotonous brown bare hill, which yielded poor crops compared to the rich plains of other provinces. The houses had mud built walls 8 inches thick, the roads were mud, and the people were covered with mud. During heavy rains the mud houses and walls fell down and wells caved in. The people remained standing.

The Department of Transportation hadn't gotten around to fixing the potholes. Someone wrote that Gansu was one "stormy sea of mountains." The "valleys" were on the roads. Caves in the mountains were "home" to those with an aversion to mud houses or who wanted to upgrade to stone exteriors.

The streets of the city were dirty; pigs ran in and out of houses. The Chinese character for "home" is made up of the character for "roof" with a "pig" under it. The roofs of the houses were curved up to trick the evil spirits from access. Apparently evil spirits were not very bright.

Chinese women did their wash in holes that had broken in the ice. They doused the clothes in the water and then whacked them with a paddle. They couldn't get them very clean because the water was the color of cocoa. Lillian wrote that a few feet away would be someone washing the roots of vegetables which had been grown in 'night soil'/feces, and just beyond that would be another person getting water for drinking.

When the central government was looking for a site for gulags to house criminals, Gansu was the chosen site. Perfect choice. Probably not many escapes during the winter. But since prisons were deplorable the motivation to flee was high year round.

Wealthy families had a "spirit wall" just inside the entry to their houses to protect the family. The belief was that spirits only traveled in straight lines, obviously they lacked sonar.

Missionaries had flower gardens. We had nasturtiums and marigolds in our yard.

Most of the cities were 5-7,000 feet above sea level. People were irritable, couldn't sleep, and had difficulty working at that elevation.

There were enough potatoes to eat, although much of the crops were traded for the next fix of opium. Soft-boiled noodles were made from wheat and topped with broth, cabbage, onions and bits of mutton, dried fish, or pork. To eat without noisily inhaling the semi-liquid was to be very rude and in the hosts eyes, unappreciative. Rice didn't grow in NW china where our family lived.

Goats provided milk for older children. Chinese mothers often nursed their babies until 3-5 years of age and they nursed David and Doris during our own mother's absence.

Young babies were bound in cloth or blankets so their arms and legs couldn't move and they were tied to the mother's back. At times Lillian took her children with her on evangelistic trips because the Chinese mothers were curious about these strange white children. Hopefully it was only our skin color that qualified us as strange. Lillian said that Richard was the first foreign child that most people in their town had seen and he spoke Chinese well so they were pleased that he could talk to them. She described "dozens of people flocking for a look at him." When the travel was far or difficult Richard remained at home with his Amah, the nanny.

Richard's Chinese Amah was afraid of the dark so Mac and Lillian had to leave a light on when they left him with her. This Amah had never seen a phonograph or heard of such a thing so was nearly overcome by it when it was demonstrated and she looked under, over, around furniture trying to figure out where the sound was coming from.

The people of Gansu lacked outward polish, appeared somewhat grumpy, and could be described as either "independent" or "difficult," depending on how you saw it. But beneath the rough exterior, they were warm at heart.

The markets were noisy with people honking, spitting, raucous laughter, and cursing. This behavior carried over to church services. They had no concept of remaining quiet in church.

Church was simple rows of boards which were 10-inches wide with 4-inch backs for the men and boys. One side was a large kang for women and children. It had a curtain drawn to provide privacy. Besides being cozy for the women, the kang provided warmth for the entire building. Women with tightly bound feet were more comfortable on the kang than the planked benches where the men sat on earth floor.

Lillian said that when they were introduced they must bow properly, remove their glasses, and ask his honorable name. He replied saying his unworthy name was Wang. He would return the favor to us and then we would ask each other's age, how many sons he had, if his worthy father was still living, and after a while we settled down to the business of the day. Removing glasses was a token of respect. It was always to be done during prayer.

Most people had two baths, once when they were born and then once after they died. Their clothing was filled with lice and the same outfit was worn until it wore out. Some of the children and adults had chronic sores on their legs and bodies from scabies.

Women kept their jet-black hair long. They oiled it and then braided it. They didn't wash it. Fine tooth combs were used to remove grime, lice and bugs before re-braiding.

In spite of the deficit in outward social charm, teachers and Chinese pastors "saved face" by making up an answer if they did not know the correct response. This provided considerable creativity to the re-telling of Bible stories, in which Noah and Moses became brothers.

Occasionally there was a wealthy family who became Christians. One woman used her home as a ministry center. Under the floor of her house lived HUGE snakes, which were spoken of with great respect "lest they be offended." They were poisonous, so not offending them made sense. The snakes survived off of the pheasants in the area.

 Speaking of "worship centers," demon worship was common in the cities, especially in southern Gansu.

Life was hard in Gansu. Mac took journeys of six weeks at a time to preach in other villages. The roads were frozen solid in the winter and clouds of dust made travel difficult in the summer. Carts got stuck in holes on the road; carefully packed supplies were dumped when Mac's mule slipped.

It wasn't just travel that was primitive. Mac and Lillian made their own soap: 8 lbs. of lime, 8 lbs. of soda, and 8 lbs. of mutton fat. Some jobs were made easier by the purchase of a donkey which cost $18.

The year that Mac and Lillian arrived in China was the beginning of motor transportation. Not for them, of course. It was also the year of the first telephone in affluent provinces. Not in Gansu.

The Chinese veneration of ancestral lineage was as much pride in who their ancestors were, as in honoring the deceased. Another source of pride was in the length of a man's fingernails. Lillian wrote that their teacher at the language school had fingernails ½" beyond his fingers which proclaimed him as in the scholarly class, and above doing ordinary work.

The coolies had a way of singing a sort of timeless song while they carried heavy loads. Lillian said that she noticed Richard carrying something across the room as a toddler chanting, "He ho, Hey ho".

In this part of China if a stranger died at your house you were responsible for his burial, which made facilitating transportation to his home when death appeared imminent a high priority, an early hospice practice about going home to die, no doubt.

Suicides were common in Gansu. Cruel mothers-in-law often abused young brides, especially if it was the 3rd wife. When life became intolerable, they jumped into the Yellow River. One city averaged 70 suicides a month, a statistic that probably was not included in the local tourist guide.

This was the place that Malcolm and Lillian Phillips served. More importantly it was the place where they came to love the people.

"He is the light that will shine upon the nations."
Luke 2:32 TLB

CHAPTER 7

Mac and Lillian served in north China at a time when it was unpopular to be an American and unsafe to be a missionary. In the beginning it was mostly rumors of danger, but soon there were actual threats against believers in the churches that Mac pastored. Bibles were burned in great piles in the street in an attempt to intimidate Chinese Christians into renouncing their faith. Church services were forbidden and the underground gatherings of small groups in various homes began. When there was a direct confrontation and a command to abandon their foreign God, Christians were tortured, publicly shot, or beheaded.

One afternoon when Mac had gone some distance to another village to preach, Lillian was at home alone with David and Doris. There was a sudden noise of soldiers shouting in the courtyard. They demanded that Lillian come out. She and the twins obeyed.

Once in the courtyard they were commanded to dig three shallow graves while the soldiers pointed guns at their heads. When the task was done David and Doris were each roped to one of Lillian's legs and Lillian's hands were tied behind her back.

The soldier in charge shouted in Chinese, "Renounce your foreign God and we will set you free!" Lillian replied, "We cannot deny the one true God. He is more powerful than your guns and if He chooses He can speak the word and we will be safe from your guns. Or, if he chooses, we will go to Heaven to live with him forever, beginning today."

The leader raised his gun and the others followed. At that exact moment the sky suddenly darkened and crashed with thunder and lightning! Lillian said that in the northern interior of China thunder and lightning were very rare. Snow and ice-yes. Torrential downpours with flashes of light and deafening thunder? Not so much.

The men trampled themselves in their eagerness to escape, convinced that the God of the missionaries had spoken. Lillian wiggled out of the wet ropes to take two "recently bathed" children back to the house for a cup of warm tea.

Hostility to Christians included young children. Teachers who were unfriendly to the Gospel continued to create impossible situations for students and did everything in their power to make life miserable for them. Heathen worship was an integral part of every school program and no child who refused to bow to the tablets and worship at the shrines could remain in school for long.

Chinese schools were quite primitive and loud. Lessons were learned by rote and each boy tried to out shout the others. Girls were too stupid to waste time trying to educate them.

Lillian wrote that although boys were much preferred, the practice of throwing away girls or putting them into the Yellow River at birth was no longer the primary method of birth control. Young girls were neglected and treated as slaves in many homes, however.

The time that girls were really valued by their parents was when they reached ages 14-16 when they were married. The bridegroom's parents were required to pay to acquire the girl for their son, the usual amount being around $20.00. This wasn't paid in cash, but in gifts of pigs or chickens. Boys and girls were engaged to be married when they were babies but were not supposed to see each other until the day of the wedding. SURPRISE!!

Some abuse was targeted exclusively to women not because they were Christians, but simply by virtue of their inferior gender. Wives were beaten into conformity. In marriage they were not companions, but utilities. They might be beaten for not producing a son, or for not providing enough wine at dinner.

As a result of this gender bias against women Lillian worked only with women and children. Mac did not preach directly to women. At times when Lillian was speaking to women, the men would gather in the next room to hear the same message from a Chinese pastor or deacon.

The Chinese in Gansu did not approve of families taking walks together as if women were equal to men. Chinese family activity was confined to the courtyard. Boys and girls were not allowed to play together outside of the home. It was the arrival of the Gospel that raised the status of women to a place of dignity. Christian parents began to view their girls in a different light and to see girls as created in the image of God.

At the time that Mac and Lillian went to China the 1,000 year old preference for women with small feet continued. Young girls had their foot bones broken, turned under, and then bandaged to prevent them from growing. The reality that this caused excruciating pain seemed secondary to the potential for 3 inch feet. It also kept the women and girls at home "where they belonged". The practice was outlawed in 1934, two years after Mac and Lillian arrived, but it wasn't really eliminated until the 1940's. In Gansu about 4/5 of the girls and all of the adult women had bound feet.

Foot binding began when girls were around 5-6 years old. In binding the great toe was left unbound and the other 4 toes were turned in. Some girls were very happy when their toes had to be amputated due to infection because that insured the "beautiful" (though horribly mutilated stumps) called "lily feet".

Unbinding was more dangerous than the initial binding because restoring tissue and blood supply was permanently lost. The demand on circulation with unbinding resulted in gangrene and infection, so some families just paid the fine rather than risk losing their girl's feet.

By the time a girl was 12 years old the foot binding process was complete and her feet would be half their normal size. Girls couldn't run and play. They could hobble, and they could get married since clearly men had no interest in girls with big feet.

The Chinese character for "good" is a combination of the letters for "woman" and "son" as though no higher good could be obtained. Male heirs were needed to carry on the ancestor worship of future generations. However, as famine came to Gansu, Chinese parents would sell one of their children for $2.00, and that included boys. Girls were sold first, of course.

Gladys Alyward, a missionary in the province next to Gansu was appointed by a government official to be the province "Foot Inspector." She traveled from village to village checking the feet of girls. A Hollywood film "Inn of the 6th Happiness" tells the story of her life in leading 100 children across the mountains to Sian during the Japanese invasion and bombing of the interior of China.

No one thought that the communists would come as far as inland Gansu, but when the news reached Mac and Lillian that a band of soldiers led by Mao Zedong was only two days travel away, they prepared to leave most of their belongings and escape. Just prior to leaving, little Kathy took a bite of a dirty potato and in a few hours was very sick with convulsions and dysentery, so the departure was delayed. By the time they could travel the communists were only one days travel away. Kathy, still very sick, was carried in a basket by the Chinese cook. Twenty-five Christians walked with Mac and Lillian and the twins and they took a small trail out of the city in hopes of avoiding Mao. Unfortunately, the communists took the same small road but decided to camp along the riverbank and cross it in the morning. A heathen man crossed the river that night and warned Mac and Lil, and they were able to get a head start.

Life in the north interior of China was becomingly increasingly dangerous for our family. Mac and Lillian and children had no permanent home for the next two years.

"I will be with you constantly until I have finished giving you all I am promising."
Genesis 28:15 TLB

"For the battle is not yours, but God's."
2 Chronicles 20:15 TLB

CHAPTER 8

Universal health care in Gansu in the 1930's predicted a likely early death. Most Chinese went first to a Chinese practitioner or herbal shop. When these did not help they came as a last resort to mission clinics, although women were fearful of displeasing men and were not permitted to walk the streets unescorted by a man to come to the clinic, so they often sent for a woman missionary through a boy or neighbor to come to them. No medical training was required. Lillian said that she was constantly surprised that anyone actually got well under her care.

Chinese were accustomed to bargaining with the doctor so that he would guarantee to get them well for so much money in so many days. If he didn't accomplish this he forfeited his pay, a health care practice that may have potential for the U.S. Some people came to the doctor only because they were curious about what caused their trouble, not to get treated.

As mentioned earlier, the Chinese in the north had an aversion to bathing (unlike other parts of China). Water was scarce and habits hard to change. In guessing the age of a person the amount of accumulated dirt was one way to judge, i.e. "He has 30 years' worth of dirt on him." One man came for surgery and the doctor scolded the nurse for not bathing him. She said the patient had refused because he had a bath nine years ago.

Another missionary in Gansu serving at the time with Mac and Lillian had no formal medical training yet successfully performed remarkable surgeries when no other option was available.

Some health practices were based on ignorance, such as giving newborn babies a good dose of castor oil. Only Richard escaped in our family. And some practices were born of necessity, such as using chopsticks for tongue depressors and as substitutes for forceps in surgery.

Some of the illnesses in Gansu came as a result of dirt, some because the idea of quarantine was viewed as a queer superstition, some as a result of inadequate hygiene or a lack of good nutrition. TB of the glands, bones, lungs was common (including for Dave and Doris); malaria was so prevalent that Chinese took it as a matter of course that they were "due" for the disease at a time each year; round worms in a protruding child's belly would reveal a tight mass of hundreds of large round worms. One girl passed 153 worms.

At times children who relied on begging for their food refused medical care for ulcers because being cured would remove their source of revenue.

The mental health of missionaries was largely addressed by a "Get a grip" philosophy. It was shameful and considered a lack of strong faith to admit to depression. Ruth Bell Graham wrote about a missionary wife in China who became depressed after the death of one of their children and the mission board wrote informing them that due to her depression they were reducing the family salary and furlough would be delayed for another year. She committed suicide.

China Inland Mission founder, Hudson Taylor, set guidelines for rest and renewal for missionaries. Ten years after Mac and Lillian arrived on the field, the standard of allowing one year of home furlough after 9 years of service became the practice. It took 3-4 months to leave the country and 2-3 months to reach an inland station, so half of the break was taken with travel.

To say that missions have changed would be an understatement, but God has not changed. His purpose has not changed. His call to make Him Lord remains.

"Forbid it Lord that I should boast,
Save in the Cross of Christ my Lord:
All the vain things that charm me most
I sacrifice them to His blood."
-Isaac Watts

CHAPTER 9

Lillian wrote that just as soon as dinner was over and she had tucked "Sonny" (that would be Richard) in bed for his afternoon nap with his trusty Amah on guard just outside the door, Mrs. Li, her Bible woman and she gathered some tracts, their Chinese Bibles, and a hymn book and tied them in a cloth ready to go. Then the two of them knelt and prayed, "Lord, lead us today." Then out of the gateway and down the narrow, dusty street the two went. Mrs. Li leading the way and Lillian following. Mrs. Li had bound feet, so they walked very slowly.

According to Chinese practice, the surname or family name (which is usually one syllable, such as Li) is written first, followed by the given (first) name. Our family surname is Pei, because it is closest to our original name of Phillips. Mac's Chinese name was Pei Li Shi.

On down the busy street Lillian and Mrs. Li jostled with the wealthy and the beggars. The cold weather had set in. They stood aside to let lumbering carts or a donkey loaded with grain pass by.

The beggars were in a different class from the very poor. Begging was a time honored occupation which one inherited and almost approached the status of a profession. Sometimes beggars collected enough money to be regarded as people of means.

Often women called out from their courtyards, "Where are you going?" and back they flung the answer, "To preach the Way." Chinese women were very friendly and Lillian found a ready welcome wherever she went.

Many children, especially boys, had a bracelet or two or a chain around their neck, intended on keeping their own spirit from escaping or another spirit from coming and taking it away. Little boys were frequently dressed as girls to fool the spirits. Girls were not worth taking.

In the middle of the crowd that soon gathered, they started their meeting. Word that a foreigner was there spread quickly, and women came from all the nearby courtyards. Lillian said that she often felt like the organ grinder and his monkey, but if she could do nothing else they could gain entrance to the courtyards and they took Jesus Christ with them. It was worthwhile to be the monkey when women were attracted to the music of the Gospel.

Some women found it hard to get past the "monkey" to listen. They crowded around her, felt her clothes, pulled on her skirt, and asked how much everything cost. Her cry went up in the midst of their chatter, "Oh, that they might see the beauty and love of Jesus."

Lillian described some of the women as dirty with heads full of lice; others had sores on their bodies.

They were not lovely to look at. But some of them were clean, especially the Muslim women. All Chinese brushed their teeth, using one brush for the whole family, of course.

Gansu women made shoes for themselves as well as shoes for their children. They did lovely work and even the most dulled (by opium) women made beautiful shoes. They made pretty aprons, bonnets, and pillows, as well. The pillows had square ends and were stuffed with cotton or something hard like rice. It seemed strange to Lillian to walk into a very poor Chinese home and see such lovely handwork.

Lillian said that there were 75,000 people in their city of Tsinchow and hundreds of little villages surrounding it filled with people who had never heard the Gospel even once.

There was one government school in Tianshui that allowed girls to attend along with boys. School started at 7 a.m. and lasted until 5 p.m. with 2 hours off for lunch.

Malcolm wrote that he would begin a two week evangelistic trip soon along with his Chinese evangelist helper. One night they planned to spend in a mission station, the rest in Chinese inns. He said they carried their own bedding with them. They didn't need much even if it was cold for they would sleep on a kang, and hope for a generous host who would keep them warm but not too warm. A young fellow who had previously traveled with Mac had a 12 inch hole burned in his bedding and woke up in the middle of the night choking on the smoke. Mac wrote that he was wearing his "wadded clothes," and that he was glad he wasn't fat since just three layers of wadding left him feeling like a quilt and he could not drop his arms to his sides.

Once, Mac was playing the accordion at a preaching hall when an earthquake hit. The crowd of 150 people fled, but Mac didn't feel the quake and was left wondering if the sudden departure was due to his impaired accordion playing talent?

During the coldest part of the winter Mac was unable to travel to other villages. Meeting places were not heated and besides, the Chinese had no time for meetings toward the end of the year. They were required to start the New Year without any unpaid bills, so there would be some frantic rushing to raise money. Bandits increased their activity in order to get enough money to pay their debts, too.

The day of Kathy's birth, February 10 happened to be on a Chinese New Year since the holiday is based on the position of the moon and not the calendar, so she was greeted with lots of fireworks and celebration. A Chinese nurse, Mrs. Wu delivered her.

"Rivers and mountains are more easily
changed than a man's nature."
-A Chinese proverb

however,

"A single spark can set a prairie on fire."
-Another Chinese proverb

CHAPTER 10
Lillian Phillips

Lillian was born in Kemmerer, Wyoming in 1905. Her parents were not Christians although her mother had attended a Lutheran Church and her father attended a Christian Church as children. Neither attended church as adults. Lillian's mother encouraged her and her sister, Margaret to attend whatever church was closest to their home, including a Mormon SS, and later Evangelical, Methodist, and, Presbyterian Sunday Schools.

When the family moved to Albany, Oregon the girls were enrolled in a Catholic school and they occasionally attended services at the Catholic Church.

One day an evangelist came to the Baptist Church in town and he conducted children's meetings every day after school, which Lillian attended. During one of the services she realized for the first time her need for a Savior. She was 14 at the time. She wanted to go forward but didn't want to do anything that would displease her parents so she asked for their permission (they said yes) and the next night while the song, "Lord, I'm Coming Home" was played she went forward and declared her faith in Christ. She said that she knew without a shadow of a doubt that she had passed from death to life. Her prayer was also a commitment to serve Christ anywhere He would lead. Her parents came to the service to observe her public confession of faith.

Until that time she had only heard one missionary and she knew nothing about becoming a missionary, but God began to plant a desire to share the Gospel in a foreign country in her heart. She also knew nothing about church attendance since she had only gone to Sunday school, but that changed after her conversion and she began attending the First Presbyterian Church. She asked the pastor if she could join the church and he said yes, next Sunday. It was at this church under the ministry of Dr. McCrossen that she began to grow in her faith. This was also the place that she would meet Malcolm, who would eventually become her husband.

During the first year after her conversion her mother and sister also became Christians and joined the church. Lillian said that the day after her conversion she took plenty of ridicule at school because the report spread quickly that Lillian had "gotten religion in a big way." She didn't care. She knew God had called her to serve Him.

She finished High School in Albany and longed to go to Bible school. She planned to enter a business college in Portland, Oregon in order to prepare for a job and save money for Bible School. The lady where she was to live broke her leg and cancelled the agreement for Lillian. She applied at Albany College but they lacked two students needed to offer the course. God gave her the verse Ruth 3:18 "Sit still, my daughter, until thou knowest how the matter will fall."

In September of that year, a large number from her home church left for Simpson Bible Institute but Lillian had no money to join them. In October after school had started the Dean at Simpson Bible Institute came to Lillian's church and led a prayer meeting. Following the service Lillian told him she hoped to attend Simpson and he asked her what she could do. She said she could do nothing. That was the reason she needed to go to Bible school, but a man in the church spoke up and said that she knew short hand. The Dean gave her an oral letter on the spot which Lillian took in short hand and then he said she could earn her tuition, room and board by being his secretary. She woke her parents up when she got home and they advised her to stick with the original plan of attending a business college, but Lillian knew that this was God's provision for her. She left the next morning at 8 a.m. but before leaving her father gave her $10, which was the most money she would have at one time all of the following year. They arrived at Simpson at midnight. Some students from Albany had prayed the previous night that God would make a way for her to come to school but they were completely shocked when they saw her at breakfast!

She worked evenings and all day Saturday for the Dean and said that she learned more in those times than she would have learned at a business college. When she needed money for personal expenses she babysat and she finished the year with no debt.

She became engaged to Mac that year at Simpson and her parents asked her to go Oregon State the second year, perhaps to dampen her enthusiasm for her handsome fiancé, as well as her commitment to become a missionary. She did not know how going to Oregon State College would help her in China, but she obeyed and it was at Oregon State that she began to love the Chinese people. She joined a foreign student club and brought home a Chinese girl every weekend from the group. She was the only Caucasian girl in the club.

At the end of the year she traveled to Seattle, married Malcolm and they both graduated from the Bible school. A missionary couple from Gansu Province was attending Simpson to complete their education and frequently invited Mac and Lillian to join them for devotional times and prayer for the loved Gansu Chinese believers. Who could have known that they would soon put faces to the names of people for whom they had prayed? It was a God-thing.

During school Mac completed his two years of required home ministry as a pastor at Shelburn, Oregon and Lillian worked for the American Sunday

School Union. After they graduated Mac became pastor in Mulketio, Washington.

They applied to the Christian Missionary Alliance (CMA) but were told that only seasoned missionaries were being sent to China due to the danger and political upheaval there.

They learned about the China Inland Mission's call for 200 young men and women willing to go to unreached sections of China and they responded. Their testimonies and pictures appeared in the China Inland's Mission (CIM) magazine, *China's Millions.*

Lillian's parents strongly opposed her going. They understood little about missions and travel to such a distant place was much different than it is today. Her parents did not want to lose contact with their brilliant grandson, either!

Shortly before time for them to sail, Lillian's mother ran her arm through the wringer of the washing machine, and soon after that Margaret, Lillian's sister, was injured in an automobile accident and broke her right arm. She was advised to go to Portland and have 6 months of daily treatment. Mac and Lillian felt they should delay leaving for China to help with the family needs and by next fall with both family members healed, they were ready to leave. The attitude of Lillian's parents had changed by then and they left with the blessing of her parents.

They sailed from Vancouver, BC, with a large group of young workers from a variety of other mission societies and were met in Shanghai, but not before she had her pockets picked and lost all of her money.

After a few days in Shanghai where they met with officials of the CIM, they left for 6 months of language school, which required two days travel up the Yangtze River. The morning before they were to leave Richard developed a high temperature and seemed quite ill, so the rest of the group went on while Mac and Lillian remained. Soon after the group left Richard revealed his new tooth and was cured of his "illness."

They were then ready to leave for Anking in Anhwei Province for language study. They would travel with another couple also headed to the school. No one spoke Chinese. They arrived at Anking early one rainy November morning. The river boat on which they were traveling could not go into the harbor and dock because the river was too shallow so little row boats pulled up alongside the steamer. The current was swift and pulled the small boats in and out with the current. Their baggage was thrown off into the small boats and then they were advised to jump, carrying Richard, of course (and, the only one who would think this leap was fun!). Mac and Richard jumped first then Lillian jumped. It was definitely a leap of faith. They were rowed to shore, still in the dark.

After unloading the baggage, all of the crew disappeared. The missionary from the language school who was supposed to meet them was nowhere in sight. The telegram telling of their expected arrival came days later. But they were not alone for long. A band of soldiers was marching down the street toward them. The soldiers were friendly and tried to talk to them. When they were not understood they spoke louder. It didn't help.

After a discussion with other soldiers, they motioned for Mac and Lillian to follow them. They felt grateful for their help in leading them to the language school. They even carried their luggage. Instead of taking them to the language school however, they took them to a large empty warehouse nearby.

Once inside the attitude of the soldiers changed dramatically. They pointed guns and bayonets at them while others cut open their trunks and broke open locks and began taking whatever they wanted. Mac and Lillian realized they had fallen into the hands of evil men.

Lillian was holding Richard when one of the guards walked by and Richard reached out to touch the shiny bayonet. The leader saw what happened and came over, held out his arms to take Richard, and Lillian's heart stopped. She handed the child over and to Lillian's amazement Richard went willingly to him. He carried Richard over to a trunk and sat down to talk to him. When he untied Richard's cap and saw Richard's red curly hair he began to laugh and ran his fingers through his hair. The other soldiers gathered around and they laughed. Richard, finding himself the center of attention joined in the laughter.

Then to Mac and Lillian's amazement the Captain gave the order to put everything back into the boxes and re-tied the ropes. He gave the order and rickshaws were called and they were escorted to the language school. When they arrived and told their story and described the soldiers they were told that the same group had recently beheaded two other missionaries.

Lillian wrote that the very hairs of our head are numbered and even the color is planned by the One who made the heaven and earth and yet to whom nothing is too small. Wherever they went in China Richard's hair was always a source of interest and Chinese people would ask Richard, "Who gave you your red hair?" Richard replied, "God gave it to me." When Richard went to Vietnam as an adult, Lillian wondered if God used his hair color again to open doors.

"The Commander of the heavenly armies is here among us." Psalm 46:7 TLB

"He closely watches everything that happens." Psalm 11:4 TLB

CHAPTER 11
Malcolm Phillips

Mac was the youngest child of seven: David, Paul, Kenneth, May and her twin James (who died at 4 months), Margaret, and finally, Malcolm. He also had 6 step-siblings by his father's first wife. As the youngest Mac had access to plenty of hand-me-downs!

His parents Maxwell and Elizabeth served as missionaries in Mexico before Mac was born. His father was an ordained Presbyterian minister and taught Greek, History, Math, and English at the University of Mexico. After returning to the States he pastored a Presbyterian Church.

Mac's father had a "hot temper" and his children in their Kansas home no doubt felt it. It may also have contributed to his divorce from wife # 1 before he married Mac's Mother.

Mac was born Jan 9, 1906 in Norman, Oklahoma and died September 30, 1947 in an industrial accident while he was working as an electrician in Albany, OR. He was 41 years old. It was just two years since the family had escaped out of China.

When he was 9 years old the family moved to Albany, Oregon for "the weather." Word about the abundant rain had apparently not leaked out as far as Oklahoma.

Mac grew up in a Christian home but made a distinct personal decision to give his heart and life to Christ. He didn't rely on being born into a "Christian family." He knew each person must choose or reject Christian faith and that salvation is not inherited.

He chose as his "life verse" Acts 13:47, "For this is as the Lord commanded when he said, "I have made you a light to the Gentiles, to lead them from the farthest corners of the earth to my salvation." He sensed at the time of his conversion that God was calling him to preach.

He attended Simpson Bible Institute in Seattle to prepare for missionary service and he began dating Lillian in his second year of school. They were married in 1927 when he was 21 years old. Both Mac and Lillian graduated from Simpson.

Mac's Father died when Mac was 14 years old His Father was 78 at the time of his death. His Mother died at age 95 years at the Oregon State Hospital where she was delightfully demented. As a student nurse Doris was assigned to the ward where her grandmother was a patient and it was obvious that everyone loved Elizabeth for her pleasant spirit.

Mac was a quiet, very bright, handsome, gentle man who was deeply loved by the Chinese he came to serve. He gave his donkey to be ridden by those he traveled with while he walked. He dressed in Chinese clothes and as much as possible he lived like the Chinese. This was a novel practice in missions during the 1930s.

When he died the church at Gangu sent a silk banner with the words:

> Missionary Pei (Chinese name for Phillips) was a pastor at Gangu for many years. He worshipped the Lord and loved the people, with excellent reputation. When he left for his own country, our church earnestly looked forward to his soon return to Gangu to pastor the church again. Not long after his departure we heard that he had arthritis, and our church prayed for him night and day. We were thankful to hear that God heard our prayers and healed him completely. But now, hearing that he went to be with the Lord we are all in shock and deep sorrow. May our banner remember and honor this faithful soul.

Then in large letters at the bottom of the banner, "The church together pulls the hearse." On the other side of the banner is written: "In commemoration of Pastor Pei and Mrs. Pei. They worshipped the Lord and loved the people. Together we bow. He sees the

Lord's glory. His journey in this desolate world is over. From now on he sees the Lord. Today in hope he has gone to heaven. No need to suffer any longer. Respectfully presented by the Gangu Christian Church." A memorial service was held at the Gangu church on December 1. The church was decorated with 50 or more white banners brought by individuals or groups. On one was written, "There is not one who does not miss him."

When our sibling group returned to Gansu in 2004 the current pastor of Gangu church wrote a beautiful poem about Mac and Lillian, in which he said, "What started well, ends well, thanks to one patriarch. What your father did for us still lasts. His name will surely be remembered."

"Let each generation tell its children what glorious things he does. I will meditate about your glory, splendor, majesty and miracles."
Psalm 145: 4-5 TLB

CHAPTER 12

The Gansu mission stations were at least one or two weeks travel apart. Mountain ranges and deserts separated them from the common life of China. To say that missionaries were on their own in isolated little pockets would be an understatement. No cell phone, no TV, no texting, no computers, no Skype, there was however, a rare piece of snail mail.

Since both the China Inland Mission and the Christian and Missionary Alliance had been working in Gansu for about 30 years before Mac and Lillian arrived, there were established churches of around 150 believers each led by Chinese pastors, but locally there were often no other English speaking missionaries for friendship and support.

Gansu borders on Inner Mongolia (where Mac and Lillian spent a short stay), Mongolia, and Tibet. Seventy percent of the land is mountainous with peaks as high as 12,000 feet. In the winter it was bitter cold and very dry. The world famous Silk Road passed through the Province. Hundreds, maybe a thousand foot drop from the plateaus led to the Silk Road below where travelers carried medicinal herbs, coal in huge lumps, wood in bundles, sacks of wheat, droves of pigs or flocks of sheep and goats…all urged on by their rough looking muleteers, shepherds, and mountain men. Travelers also included Hindu merchants with silk and pearls. Mohammedan pilgrims returning from Mecca, and bearded traders from Russia brought high boots and girdles, high hats and turbans, and long trains of camels.

The Silk Road ran alongside the Yellow River, which flowed through the southern part of Gansu into the heart of central China. The river began in the high Himalayan Mountains and flowed to the plains of China's breadbasket. This mighty river frequently flooded its banks and devastated villages. It extends 4,000 miles and is the 5th longest river in the world. At Lanzhou, the capitol of Gansu, the river is still at 5,250 feet elevation.

Traders along the sand blown desert brought goods from Persia, India, Arabia, and the Mediterranean, but they also brought cultures and religions, primarily Islam as they arrived by camel caravan, crossed the Yellow River and took the Silk Road to Sian, the heart of China. Their religious practices marked them as distinct from the dominant Han Chinese people. Malcolm ministered to Muslims, Han, Tibetans, and anyone else who he met.

Although these Muslims adopted Chinese dress they had distinct physical characteristics. The men wore closely cropped moustaches and bushy beards with a white skullcap, indicating that the man had made his pilgrimage to Mecca, or a black skullcap, indicating he hadn't.Silk veils hid the women's faces.

Muslims lived peacefully with the Han. They owned shops, served in the military, and found places of leadership in government. They rejected pork and instead they ate mutton, lamb, or goat meat. They had strict rules about cleanliness and bleeding animals, which were quite similar to Jewish Kosher laws.

Muslims maintained exclusive communities to practice their faith outside the walled gates of the city. At the hospital in Lanzhou, where Mac regularly visited when he was in the city, there was a separate ward for Muslims. There were 2-3 million of them in Gansu in the years before Mac and Lillian arrived. About 10,000 were buried in a terrible earthquake 12 years earlier. The Han Chinese knew that earthquakes were "messages from the gods, and finding who was responsible for offending these gods was critical." Missionaries were the logical prime suspects.

In the southern part of Gansu it was six days travel to reach a doctor at Lanzhou. So much for "early intervention."

In addition to the hospital at Lanzhou, there were crowded markets with foreign cigarettes, Tibetan butter, shoe and hat shops, furs, velvet, satin, and white fox for sale.

Most poor families in Gansu (which would include our family) survived the bitterly cold winters bundled in their layers of padded clothes, sometimes as many as 10 layers. People looked like chubby stick figures.

Some poor Chinese lived day and night on their kang, the brick bed that provided the only source of heat in the house. The kang was used throughout northern China and in the room for living and sleeping; it took up ¾ of the space. An opening to the outside wall allowed a fire to be built under the bed. The fuel was usually animal manure mixed with straw and leaves. Since there was no chimney the smoke, putrid odor and grime penetrated the air. Sort of like sleeping next to the cat litter box, only a LOT worse. Our family slept on a kang in Gansu, which used coal as the source of heat and therefore less smell, but the Environmental Protection Agency would definitely label the fumes undesirable. The air was so smoke-filled that seeing across the room was impossible.

When our family traveled and stayed at native inns, the amount of heat on the kang was determined by the generosity of the host. If he was generous, we roasted. If he was stingy, we froze. Even on a well-heated kang, the boiling water in teapots would be frozen solid by morning in winter.

All travelers arriving at the inn that day shared the same kang. Men, women, children, strangers, officials, and peasants, all side by side on the hard platform. UN-invited "guests" included various vermin, which infected the kang.

Mac and Lillian became accustomed to chipping off bits of frozen bread and thawing it in their mouths before they could eat it. Breakfast consisted of frozen bread and scraps of frozen meat or cheese. Sometimes it was mutton broth, an item not likely to sell well at Starbucks.

From the outside of the inn camels could be seen munching from their feed bags, along with mules that had carried travelers over treacherous narrow trails with sharp precipices. Safety for travelers was completely dependent on the sure-footed steps of the mules, which at times were NOT so sure-footed and managed to dump Dave and Doris out of their baskets, although to their credit, they never sent them down any steep cliffs. Whatever lack of brain function is present in the twins cannot be blamed on mule-malpractice.

City gates were closed at dusk and re-opened at dawn. When danger threatened, the gates were closed at any hour. To be caught outside the gates at night was to become prey to bandits.

Southern Gansu was cultivated by large irrigation water wheels that carried river water through bamboo troughs 15-25 feet above the river. The water traveled through trenches, bamboo buckets filled and sloshed leading to canals, which provided water for crops of potatoes, soybeans, mustard and peppers. The common waterways became contaminated and carried disease.

Sanitation was minimal. Trench latrines were emptied every night by the "night soil" coolies and were then sold to farmers and gardeners for fertilizer. Vegetables became easy carriers of dysentery.

Private bathrooms were non-existent. Usually men and boys went around the corner. Children wore split pants and squatted. Women and foreigners were slightly more private. The chamber pot was kept by the kang and was emptied into the night soil in the morning.

Life in Gansu would not be recommended in a Travel and Leisure magazine. It would be more difficult than anything Mac and Lillian had ever imagined.

"Anyone who wants to follow Me must put aside his own desires and conveniences and carry his cross with him every day and keep close to Me."
Luke 9:23 TLB

CHAPTER 13

Missionary work never happens in a political vacuum and China was on the brink of chaos.

Ten years before Malcolm and Lillian arrived the communist party of China held its first national meeting in Shanghai. It was held in secret. The year was 1921.

Dr. Sun Yat-sen was disappointed with the lack of support for his new movement from the United States and turned to Russia as an ally. He also had the support of peasants in south China and they began their "Long March" of 6,200 miles to the North, a distance that may be exaggerated.

Sun Yat-sen's successor as party leader was Chiang Kai-shek, but in 1927 Chaing turned against the Communist party to begin his own movement and Mao Zedong became leader of the Communists.

By the time Mac and Lillian arrived in China Japan had seized Manchuria and renamed it "Manchukuo"; Muslims were revolting; and there was famine with thousands of people being fed every day by the missionaries. Parents were giving their children away in an attempt to keep them alive. The political tension was almost at a breaking point. Chiang Kai-Shek in his attempt to destroy the communists and to push the nation under his rule had made a war zone of most of China. China was a dangerous place for missionaries!

For Mac and Lillian language school was over and they would travel to the large city of Tianshui which was to be their home for the next year while they gained some experience. There was an established church of about 150 Christians in the city.

Shortly after they arrived a new Mayor took over. He was both anti-Christian as well as anti-foreigner. Up until that time the church had no trouble of any kind from the city officials, but the new Mayor announced at his first meeting that he was opposed to the work of missionaries and he intended to drive them out of town, destroy the church and cause the Chinese to return to idol worship.

So, the first Sunday the Mayor sent soldiers to the front gate of the compound which housed the church as well as the home of Mac and Lillian. As Christians came to church the soldiers took their Bibles and hymn books from them, tore them to shreds and threw them in a pile in the courtyard. Many pleaded with the soldiers to allow them to keep their Bibles as they were very precious to them, but the soldiers had their orders and not one was spared. After everyone had arrived the Bibles were set on fire.

The Mayor himself arrived and ordered the people to go inside and standing behind the pulpit he told them that they were to stop following the foreign God and if they came back the next Sunday they would be beaten. If they came the 3rd week they would be shot. It was not expected to be a good marketing tool for church growth!

He dismissed the group and he and his men left, but the Christians stayed behind to decide what to do and to pray. They decided that instead of coming to the church where they would be disturbed they would meet in four different homes in the city.

The next week they met and although they did not have Bibles the Christians knew many long passages of Scripture by heart and they sang the words. They reminded each other of the verses in Romans 14:7-8 (TLB), "We are not our own bosses to live or die as we might choose. Living or dying, we follow the Lord. Either way, we are his."

So when the soldiers went to the church and found no worshippers they believed their plan had been a success.

On Monday attacks began on the missionaries; stores were ordered not to sell them food, a guard was set at the compound gate so they could not leave and no one could come in. But in the early morning hours when the guard went to sleep, Christians slipped in and out with food.

No mail was allowed to go out or be received. Mac and Lillian were cut off from the outside world. Christian homes were being stalked one by one; men were threatened with loss of jobs if they did not renounce their faith in Christ. The cook who worked for Mac and Lillian was beaten.

On Wednesday the Mayor held a meeting and each family was to send one representative. He ordered them to march to the Catholic hospital and destroy it. Hundreds of people broke medicine bottles, windows, ruined instruments, and pulled patients out of their beds to the floor. Of course all of the supplies at the hospital were for the good of the people of the city.

After leaving the hospital they were told to go to the compound where Mac and Lillian lived, but some Christians who had seen what was happening rushed to tell them.

The soldiers had provided their own early warning system, however. As they marched along the side of the compound Mac and Lillian could hear them chanting, "Down with the foreigners. Down with the running dogs (servants) of the foreigners." The front gate had been left open knowing they would only knock it down if it had been locked. When they reached the gate the leader led in more chants, but suddenly pouring rain came down and the soldiers scattered, drenched and afraid. Again, God used rain to protect his saints.

"What heathen god can give us rain? Who but you alone, O Lord our God, can do such things as this?"
Jeremiah 14:22 TLB

Children also suffered persecution. A picture of Sun Yat-sen was posted in each school room and the teacher announced that beginning that day every child was to bow in worship to the picture. The Christian children refused. The next day at school the teacher said that at each hour they would stop to worship their glorious leader, Sun Yat-sen, and anyone who refused would have his head cracked on the head of another Christian student. Christian children said they could bow only to the true God whose name was Jesus. As promised, their heads were cracked on the heads of other students.

On the third day of school the children were told that they could do anything they wanted to do to the Christian students with no punishment. By then the teacher was feeling guilty so on the fourth day, little Samuel, a Christian boy in the school was invited to tell a Bible story and every day after that Samuel told a story about Jesus. The teacher became a Christian herself soon after that.

In addition to the local persecution, Communist soldiers arrived in the city and took everything that Mac and Lillian owned except the clothes they were wearing. Later they again lost all of their possessions to Japanese soldiers. Possessions were quickly becoming un-important....and, non-existent.

With all of the suffering the church began to grow. The small church of 50 grew into hundreds. The mayor publicly lamented, "The more I persecute them, the stronger they become." Years later after Mac and Lillian returned to the U.S. this Mayor became a Christian and returned to the church he had persecuted to give his testimony and begin a life of serving Christ.

Just prior to Mac and Lillian's arrival in Tianshui, some Muslims had raided the city and killed many people. There were two doctor brothers in town and one of them was killed. The other brother's face was badly mutilated. Later when Mac was preaching, at the close of a service Dr. Wu, the surviving doctor came forward and handed his scalpel to Mac saying he wanted to dedicate his knife to serving Christ. A stranger had come to church that night. He carried a hidden dagger that he said he intended to use to kill Dr. Wu, but now he wanted to ask forgiveness and surrender his dagger. Mac stood at the front of the church holding in one hand a scalpel and in the other hand a dagger.

"For whatever God says to us is full of living power: it is sharper than the sharpest dagger."
Hebrews 4:12 TLB

CHAPTER 14

The political turmoil in north China was expanding.
Japanese soldiers destroyed everything in sight as
they entered villages with their machine guns. They
"scorched the earth" with bombs as their planes flew
low over cities. They boarded up houses with women
and children inside and then set the houses on fire.
Finding food to avoid starvation was increasingly a
challenge. People fled from the towns and hid in
remote caves. Gladys Aylward, missionary in the
province next to Gansu began her trek across the
mountains with the 100 children she wanted to deliver
to safety.

Missionaries needed to escape from Gansu and the
only possible transport would be on rafts of goat,
sheep, or pig skins down the Yellow River. Traveling
by any other means was not an option, and the CIM
headquarters had ordered them to leave. It was 1935.
Just a few years before the Mission had required the
missionaries to evacuate in the same way avoiding
the tedious, dangerous journey over the mountains.

The rafts were made in Lanzhou, capitol city of
Gansu. Missionaries left their possessions, not that
Mac and Lillian had much to leave. Each raft would
hold 15-16 adults and several children, 2 boatmen
and a servant, altogether about 23 people. A cook
made a mud fireplace at the rear of the boat. A dining
area with mats, sleeping quarters with canopies, and

piles of luggage completed the structure. They brought live chickens so eggs would be available, plus rice, oatmeal, and potatoes. The chickens would be killed at the end of the trip and eaten.

Each day the rafts stopped at land and Richard and Kathy played with frogs, beetles, lizards, and prairie dogs while the rafts were blown up, a task that needed to be done 2X day in order to keep the 1,000 rafts of skin afloat. River pirates frequently stopped the rafts to demand $30 as "fees." They would need to navigate whirlpools, torn skins on the raft, and an occasional small earthquake as they passed through the famous gorges.

Multiple groups of missionaries fled from Lanzhou for the 1-3 week trip down the Yellow River to the safety of Inner Mongolia, and that included our family.

By 1937, the year David and Doris were born at Yudaoho, Shansi, eight miles north of Fenyang, the Japanese had set tank traps and other obstacles on roads. They took care of their causalities at their own hospitals. When Japanese soldiers passed a group of farmers working in fields they used them for target practice. Women and children were shot in cold blood or killed when they accidently stepped on grenades. In China a person's leg did not belong to the individual, it belonged to his family, so he could not agree to an amputation without his family's consent.

By July, 1937, one month before Dave and Doris were born the political situation was very dangerous. Only people, who could classify themselves as "Chinese Nationalists", or, as Japanese military leaders, were safe. Roving guerrilla bands harassed railways at night. Beheadings were common and heads were displayed on the city walls, 10-20 at a time. Mac and Lillian were in Shanghai in a car right behind Madame Chiang Kai Shek when a hand grenade was thrown at her.

Following the war most men cut off their queue (pigtail), which had been a symbol of subservience to the Manchu, but this was less common in northwest China. Some missionaries encouraged cutting the pigtail to state that Christians were free from the bondage of sin.

One year later in 1938 Richard entered Chefoo, a boarding school for the children of missionaries. He was 6 years old.

"If the Lord is with us, why has all this happened to us? And where are all the miracles our ancestors have told us about? The Lord said, "I will make you strong! Go." Judges 6:13-14 TLB

"My power shows up best in weak people." 2 Corinthians 12:9 TLB

CHAPTER 15

The Great Wall of China was built more than 2,000 years ago and is about 3,700 miles long. A portion of it stretched into Gansu, one of the 23 provinces. It was built to keep out the horses of the Tartans, because men could climb over the wall but not their horses. Without horses the men were not strong.

The Galloping Horse of Gansu was one of the most famous sculptures found in China. Horses were important for the rich and famous. Our family rode donkeys.

When Lillian was 9 months pregnant with the twins in 1937 she rode a donkey for two weeks to where doctors often vacationed at a mission retreat center. There were no doctors present, however, when the twins arrived two hours apart. Riding on a donkey, while nine months pregnant with twins, has been known to induce labor, or at least discomfort. The birth of twins was not a welcomed event for the Chinese. What possible good could come from TWO mouths to feed?

During Mac and Lillian's last term in China they worked in the city of Gangu. There was a church in the city and three outstations. Mac and Lillian added two more outstations during their time in the city. An out station had ten or more Christians, a place of worship, and a leader. The Chinese leaders adapted

Biblical stories to the Chinese way of life, for example, coolies helped the prodigal son with his baggage when he returned home, etc. Malcolm and Lillian visited each of these outstations to preach and encourage the believers. In the beginning they rode by donkey, but when that became too expensive they rode by bicycle, which took less fuel, but more energy.

David and Doris rode in baskets in the front and rear of the bike, or, on either side of a borrowed donkey, but always in baskets. Several times on each trip the donkey would lie down and roll over dumping the twins out on to the road. The road was always a narrow trail carved out of the mountains.

The Christians would be waiting at the church with hot tea and a warm welcome. The singing left a lot to be desired, but what it lacked in quality, it more than made up for in volume. There was little stigma to belting it out without the ability to keep on tune here. The Biblical references to, "making a joyful noise" were written for the Gansu Christians. Lillian wrote about hearing a Chinese choir sing the, Hallelujah Chorus, during their time in China. She said it was beautiful. None of the singers would have been from Gansu!

Gansu was a preacher's paradise because the longer you preached the more they appreciated it. If you preached under two hours, they thought you cheated them. "You came all the way from the city and only preached 1 ½ hours?"

After the service they were invited to a home for a bowl of noodles, and later they visited the sick, or, assisted a new believer in destroying his idols. Lillian would hold a special meeting for women and children.

Then the bell would ring and it was time for another meeting to begin. The Christians had used the break to invite non-believers to "come and see the foreigner's children", so there would be a large gathering for the later service.

Chinese valued paper so they were eager for the tracts which the missionaries provided. Throwing away paper was an offense. It was common to see a poor old man gathering scraps of paper in a bag to be properly buried. He was storing up merit for the next world.

After one of these outstation visits, a man asked if he could come and live in our home and cook for us. He had been previously employed as a cook in a restaurant and was very skilled. When he arrived he was not a Christian, but before long he became a follower of Jesus along with his wife and children. He pierced his ear as a sign that he was committed to serving our family forever, so when it was time for Mac and Lillian to leave China it was hard for him to comprehend why he had to remain in Gansu.

Another helper volunteered to weed our garden during a time when robbers climbed over our fence and took the growing food for our family. We had a dog which barked as a warning initially, but they poisoned the dog. The volunteer gardener was completely blind, but an expert in sorting weeds from plants and he worked all night. Scaling the wall was met with a loud scream by the blind man with sensitive ears. The robbers decided they were less hungry than they had originally thought they were.

"If such men walk in darkness without one ray of light, let them trust the Lord, let them rely upon their God."
Isaiah 50:10 TLB

"The people who walk in darkness
shall see a great Light."
Isaiah 9:2 TLB

CHAPTER 16

The south of Gansu which borders Tibet has a population of Muslims, Salars, Tibetans, and aborigines, all under Chinese rule. Each race spoke its own language with varying dialects. Many centuries ago most of Gansu Province belonged to Tibet.

One sect of tribal people had extraordinary hair which was never cut or combed or washed and was worn in a heavy coil on the top of the head protected from rain and dust by a cap. It was thick as a man's arm and hung almost to the ground. The people were poor, dirty, and uneducated. Most of the mountain people had lice. Life for Mac and Lillian was complicated by the diverse social habits, manners and customs of each of these sects.

In the mountain ranges north of Lanzhou were towns where no one had heard the Gospel. These people had no shops, no markets, no inns, no food stalls. Missionaries would go dressed like mountaineers and carry all the food they would use, along with books and bedding.

West of Lanzhou was the famous Thousand Buddhist Temples, and caves as well as the Labrang Monastery, one of the largest outside of Tibet.

Monks lived there with supreme hypocrisy and they fostered evil and moral decadence. There was also a lower moral standard in people living near the southern border of Gansu. Tibetans had a reputation as thieves and burglars.

A large orphanage for girls near the Mongolian border was notorious for throwing away girls or killing them at birth.

At the Kum Bum Butter Festival a huge Buddha image was sculptured from hard Tibetan butter and partying was interspersed with religious rituals. The Tibetans brought in yak meat and hardened yak butter and bales of yak and sheep wool.

A path led to the lamasery where pilgrims went chanting prayers and spinning prayer wheels, some measuring the distance with their bodies by repeated prostrations on the dust path hoping to gain merit in the 68 ways of Buddhist salvation.

Some of these monks were curious about the foreign missionary and his teaching and would say, "If your teaching is better than mine then I will be your disciple; if mine is better than yours then you will be my disciple." But many monks gathered the Bibles and tracts and publicly burned them. For most of these monks the possession of a single page of Scripture was punishable by the loss of the right hand.

In addition to the many Tibetans in southern Gansu, there were numerous Muslims. They were not allowed to live inside the city walls, so they planted communities just outside the gates. They were considered smart merchants and good at bargaining. The main thing that set the Muslim apart from the other Chinese was abstinence from and hatred for idolatry.

Muslims accepted the virgin birth of Christ and his miracles. One important fact was left out however and that is, Islam taught that on the way to the cross Jesus was caught up alive into heaven by a rescuing angel. They denied the death and resurrection of Christ and therefore his saving power.

A funny story took place during the 5th century when Mohammedans were looking for wives. The Emperor ordered a great theatrical production and reserved seats for all of the young maidens. The Muslim men were hiding behind curtains and at a signal they sprang out and captured a bride. Surprisingly, the plan worked well and the Chinese accepted the Muslims. E-Harmony is considering adopting this match-making system.

During the time that Mac and Lillian worked in Gansu they observed that once all of the religious duties had been performed the Muslims felt more or less at liberty to do whatever they pleased including lying, adultery, cheating, cursing, murder and heartless arrogance. All were common and accepted behaviors.

Women in Muslim communities had no liberty and no rights. They were seriously abused by their husbands. Divorce occurred only at the husband's decision and could be for a trivial offense.

The Salars, a sect of Muslims were the true trouble makers of Gansu. They were the most bigoted and intolerant, the most unapproachable and resistant to outside influence. They had a history of cannibalism and hunted other human beings or dogs to eat.

Malcolm and Lillian served in four different provinces in the north interior of China. When they were forced to move suddenly to seek sanctuary in another city or village, they immediately sought out ministry opportunities. When they were in Lanzhou, capitol of Gansu, Mac preached at the hospital every day. He "bloomed where he was planted" for 13 years.

He also taught a Bible study which required crossing the Wei River at times without a raft, so he waded in waist high water. A church developed from that Bible study and on our return visit to Gangu in 2004 we were warmly welcomed there. It was clear that Mac and Lillian were loved!

Mac and Lillian had reached out to all of these people. Tibetans, Muslims, tribes people all lived in Gansu and were the community to which God had called them to love and serve.

"Red and yellow, black and white, they are precious in his sight...."

Jesus Loves the Little Children
Words by: C. Herbert Woolston

CHAPTER 17

Every missionary kid in the China Inland Mission knew the day would come when he would be sent away to school. Amahs who took care of Richard and Kathy would grieve the loss of their loved charges. Most MK's left with one toy and a couple of books. They were ages 5 or 6 years depending on the travel needs of their parents. In a perfect world they would see their parents at Christmas, unless their parents were assigned to Gansu, which made travel too difficult, and 40 days travel too long for a Christmas visit. Hopefully, they could have a summer visit, but that would be in a perfect world, and almost nothing in China was perfect in 1936.

If the map of China's coast looked like a teakettle, where the spout joined the kettle would be the city of Chefoo in northern Shandong Province. The setting had rocky rugged hills with gentle slopes to the beach. The experience that would follow for Richard and Kathy would be sometimes rocky and always rugged.

Mac and Lillian did what they believed to be in the best interest of Richard and Kathy in sending them to Chefoo where they would receive an excellent education in a Christian environment. It was what the Mission expected of two full time missionaries. Childcare tasks needed to be done by someone else. We cannot apply today's knowledge about the needs of young children to those days 75 years ago, but the impact of being left in an institutional-type setting at such a young age cannot be minimized, either.

Children arrived at the school by various means. Some by spring-less mule-litter travel which was tiring. Sitting on top of freight while snorting swirling dust, was not pleasant. Some came by truck, but that was expensive. For some, including Richard, the trip included a 48-hour boat ride from Tientsin. Lillian wrote that Richard was disappointed that the waves didn't tip the boat over far enough. His parents did not share his opinion.

For other children the journey to school would be by ship with a coolie carrying the child's belongings on board and then school escorts took over responsibility for the final lap of the journey.

The south China coast was notorious for pirate activity and young boys hoped they would be so lucky. Escorts and parents hoped they would NOT.

Returning from furlough in 1939 Mac and Lillian and the four children needed to take the long way around to enter China due to the political upheaval and that included a stop in Vietnam. While they were there David pulled a kettle of boiling hot water over himself, scalding 1/6th of his body surface. Even though he made a rapid recovery without scars, still it was a painful experience. It was the Lord's provision at that time that a Chinese Red Cross doctor was at the Inn, and he was on the spot within two minutes to provide first aid.

Mac and Lillian left Richard and Kathy at Chefoo and told the children they would see them in two years. Actually it was almost five years before they were re-united. Kathy was 5 and Richard was 9 years old.

Tension between the Japanese and Chinese armies throughout China continued to increase. It became evident that Japan's benevolent words were in contrast to its actions. Japan forcefully colonized and ran roughshod over its new territories, destroying its leadership and enslaving its people. They were causing trouble in the countryside including the interior of Shensi, Shansi and Gansu. Many missionaries were evacuated to the south and arrived in Shanghai, Mac and Lillian among them.

Scores of refugees too, poured into Shanghai with all of their worldly goods packed around them on rickshaws. Shanghai had a modern train station, elegant streetcars, and skylines of art deco buildings. Foreigner hotels did not allow Chinese to stay unless employed by a western family, and signs read, "No dogs or Chinese allowed".

Japan had a national craving for respect among the world's movers and shakers. They believed the British had gained power by military force, and so could they.

By July of 1937 Japan invaded Peking but did not bomb it because it had financial interests there, but the city fell anyway and the Japanese were in control. At first this was only a war between the Japanese and the Chinese. It didn't involve the Americans or British. That all changed, of course with the bombing of Pearl Harbor in Hawaii.

The Japanese made amazing advances throughout the country and the Chinese were not prepared to fight them. Chinese men and boys were forced to fight in the Japanese army and if they deserted the entire family would be killed.

This was the setting for Richard and three years later for Kathy when they arrived at Chefoo. Henry Luce, former editor and owner of *TIME* magazine, and a former student at Chefoo wrote, "I loved Chefoo and I hated it." Most students who graduated from Chefoo highlighted the fun experiences and the quality of education. Amnesia is a wonderful thing.

Chefoo was modeled after the English public school system. Teacher training about the emotional needs of children was not a part of the curriculum. Discipline was stern. Spinsters who were well intended but emotionally cold and unable or unwilling to demonstrate affection provided much of the day-to-day care. The Bible was the standard of conduct, especially the, "spare the rod, spoil the child" part.

Missionary parents relied on Mark 10:29-30 when Jesus said, "Truly I say to you there is no one who has left house or brothers or sisters or mother or father or CHILDREN or lands for my sake and the Gospel who will not receive a hundred fold...." Mothers reminded each other of Hannah who gave Samuel to the Lord when he was only three years old and they found comfort in knowing that he overcame the negative forces in his life to become a positive force for God.

For some children the deep and lasting spiritual experience compensated for the detrimental emotional experience. For others, the separation from parents during vulnerable childhood years along with the emotional harshness of life at the boarding school left scars. Children of missionaries believed their experience was normal and many said that they only missed their parents in the beginning. Kathy's chosen Bible verse, "For if my father and mother should abandon me, you would welcome and comfort me." She wasn't the only five-year old to choose this verse.

On Kathy's refrigerator, 75 years later, is the Scripture,
"To enjoy your work and to accept your lot in life that is indeed a gift from God. The person who does that will not need to look back with sorrow on his past, for God gives him joy."
Ecclesiastes 5:20 (TLB)

CHAPTER 18

The Chefoo School experience for Richard and Kathy was a "before and after" story; before the invasion of Japanese troops and afterwards when children were led to concentration camps. The "before" was stark. The "after" was brutal.

The school for missionary children was founded in 1881 by Hudson Taylor, and in part was built from the wreckage of a two ships in the bay. It opened with 12 students but by the time Richard and Kathy enrolled there were 350 students. The school was acclaimed as the "finest school east of Suez", with "finest" meaning that the academic standards were the highest.

One half of the students came from CIM workers, 25% from other missions, and 25% from families of business or Chinese government service workers. A graduate from Chefoo was aged 16 or 17 years and if the student passed the Oxford exams with 75% he had passed the Oxford University entrance requirements. Of course Chefoo students passed.

Loyalty to everything British dominated Chefoo. Americans were second-rate. "After all, he's an American", explained it all. Students memorized the Kings of England and on British holidays the flag was hung above the dining room door. At the Prep school, a teacher, (American, of course), was suspected of wearing lipstick in private, a sin right up there with playing cards and reading secular books.

There was no central heating in the dorms for the youngest children. The school was heated with a black potbelly stove. "Form" was the British school system equivalent for Grade levels. Prep school forms were for students through age 10 and then Boys or Girls School followed.

Punishment at the Prep School consisted of caning (the use of a switch) or thin bamboo cane to inflict pain on a child's outstretched hand. Boys were expected to bend over and hold their ankles to receive the cane strokes. Lifebuoy soap on an old toothbrush applied to the mouth encouraged telling the truth or, at least not talking when the teacher wanted silence. When a boy began to bully younger children he was required to punch a concrete pillar. Small infractions were treated like major crimes and children were held up as "thieves and sinners." They were made to write letters to parents confessing their sins, which were humiliating and painful. These minor sins were held against students for their rest of their years at Chefoo. So much for grace and forgiveness.

Students who didn't confess were placed in solitary and given only bread and water until they confessed. It was better to confess to something you hadn't done than to go hungry. There was no punishment for lying about crimes you had NOT committed. Punishment was often in front of the whole school, which added to the shame.

One former student wrote, "Without the traits of intelligence or beauty, students had difficulty. For the strong, Chefoo was a fine happy experience, for the weak, it was potentially a devastating experience." Surprisingly, after the arrival of the Japanese and the school leaders experienced their brutality, corporal punishment of students was changed to the removal of privileges.

Left-handed students were expected to conform to right hand writing. Clothing at the school was a big deal. Everyone wore uniforms. During the winter when it was bitter cold students wore dog-fur stockings, pigskin shoes, thick blue pull-overs and wool bloomers. In the summer Richard wore white shirts and khaki pants with long cotton knee socks and sandals. On April 1, students changed to summer clothes regardless of the weather. The rule was a challenge of mind over (freezing) matter, encouraging students to "think warm thoughts" in spite of the thermometer reading.

A cobbler came to the school and drew the foot outline of each student on brown paper and in a few days the finished product would be delivered.

Each morning before the students woke up a servant would come and light the fires, allowing drinking water time to thaw. One time the ocean water was frozen 5 miles out to sea and people went out on solid ice in rickshaws to meet passengers in the outer harbor. Tooth brushing mugs were filled with water and placed on window ledges so that children could have "popsicles" to lick.

Christmas break was for two months and most children went home, but the rest stayed at school and played hockey, went sledding or spent time reading.

Of course, some students suffered from homesickness and loneliness. What was gained academically was lost emotionally. To survive at Chefoo was to conform. Some students spent 12 years at Chefoo and although they had visits from their parents the attachment to them faded in time. Some students did not see their parents for years at a time. "There are two people who are my mother and father but I don't know them and they don't know me."

Some parents left children at Chefoo and went to the U.S. for furlough. When parents visited the school they stayed in a spacious wooden guesthouse or rented a cottage for $20 month plus $5 for furniture.

Girls were not allowed to talk to boys other than their brothers; however this didn't prevent swapping brothers on the 1-½ mile walk home from the Anglican Union Church. Students found other ways to adapt to the rigid standards. For example when students were sent to their rooms for naps a "sentry" was posted so that a teacher with a slipper in hand would find all of the students "asleep." No wonder that at the end of Richard's first day at school when he was asked by his parents what he had learned he said he'd learned okay, but not from the teachers!

During the summer students whose parents served in Gansu remained at Chefoo. It was too far to travel to inland China.

Most of the boys and many of the girls could swim 1-3 miles with ease by the time they left Chefoo. Every day was swimming day except Sunday during summer months. The method of teaching swimming was barbaric. Ten boys would be taken out in a boat. The instructor would announce, "Do you want to be thrown in, jump in, or dive in?" Usually the reply was jump in. The boy then swallowed salt water and just before he thought he would drown, a senior boy would grab him and tow him to the boat where he would flop in like a sack of fish. There he would sit, coughing water out of his lungs and watching his fellow victims. Soon his turn would come again, this time the instructor would provide some instructions: kick your feet, keep your mouth closed. And with this, the boy's swimming career had begun.

Students were denied the opportunity to learn the Chinese language and culture. Teachers felt their main goal was to prepare them for their English speaking homelands. They were distanced from Chinese servants at Chefoo too, because they couldn't speak the language. The Mandarin that Richard and Kathy learned as young children was forgotten.

As mentioned, students woke up at 5 a.m. when a servant came to remove ashes from the potbelly stoves and re-build a fire. By 6 a.m. the rising bell sounded and the Master of the day called for inspection to check for sniffles, coughs, earaches. After that, students ran to their cold shower.

At 7 a.m. a servant went through the hall hitting the "Silence Gong" and 15 minutes of "Quiet Time" followed. At 7:15 students marched to the dining room for hot cereal, a hard-boiled egg and "scrape" (molasses or jelly over toast).

Seating in the dining room was by number and rotated each day one space so that on rare occasions a student might sit across from a sibling.

After breakfast, the wardrobe mistress stood at her station while students paraded by her. She carefully inspected each one for neatness and the right uniform.

After inspection and before going to class students assembled for morning prayers. Heavy emphasis was placed on memorizing Scripture, so later when their

Bibles were taken away; the children knew a great deal of Bible verses by heart.

Even free time was structured. Athletics were required. One class period was used for writing letters. The teacher suggested topics and letters were censored.

Without the presence and warmth of parents students accepted the rigid boarding school way of life.

The school, like the CIM practiced dependence on Divine guidance in every situation and for every need. The mission policy was never to ask for contributions of any kind, but to pray that God would meet each need.

The staff was self-disciplined, austere and lacking in curiosity about in the wider world. But they were sincerely committed to God's direction. Students knew that God's hand was over them whatever happened. It was a foundation they would need soon.

"He alone is my refuge."
Psalm 91:2 TLB

"God is our refuge and strength,
a tested help in times of trouble."
Psalm 46:1 TLB

CHAPTER 19

Life in the little beach town of Chefoo (later re-named, Yantai) was busy with normal activity. Men pulled rickshaws of loaded carts or pushed wheelbarrows. The word "coolie" came from the Chinese characters "ku" and "li" meaning bitter strength. Open stall markets specialized in the sale of one item: tea, cloth, and, money changing. Peddlers bargained for fruit or vegetables. You could get a haircut on the street or a bowl of noodles. A treat of a sweet package of rice and dates steaming hot and wrapped in leaves was the equivalent of a trip to McDonalds. Maybe better. Russian and Filipino entertainers performed at saloons and cabarets when a ship was anchored in the bay.

Chinese were not heavy drinkers, but most of them took a nip occasionally. The whiskey was cheap. A person could get drunk on 3 cents U.S. Mac wrote that he used the stuff to light his kerosene gas lamp and also pressure stove. Hospitals bought the whiskey in place of alcohol for sterilizing.

It was a different world inside Chefoo School where the corner stone read: "Hitherto hath the Lord helped us. This foundation is laid to commemorate the faithfulness of God in connection with the China Inland Mission School founded in AD 1881 for the education of children of missionaries. The Lord will provide."

The school was built like an ivy-covered grand old English boarding school. Education was taken seriously, but so were sports. There were tennis courts, racquetball courts, parallel and uneven bars, a jungle gym, a roller-skating area, and a soccer field. Competition in athletics, boat racing, swimming, and sand sculpturing contests were all a part of life as a student at Chefoo.

In 1938, 22 young men came to Chefoo to live while they did language study. They became known as the, "Sons of the Prophets," which explained their preaching services, but not so much their organization of concerts, and sporting events, unless their prophetic gifts included projection of sport team winners! They had a huge impact on the school and its sports teams.

The playgrounds were divided for boys and girls. Going to the beach was a daily summer activity. Sometimes grown-ups let students dangle their feet out of a rowboat. The water was very clear showing the sea bottom with fish darting among the seaweed or transparent jellyfish. The Chefoo crest was a dolphin.

There were pens on the property for goats and chickens and some children took care of gardens. Students performed Shakespeare's plays and offered musical performances. Visitors from other ports often visited the school and provided lectures and concerts in the evening.

The setting of the school at the beach, the participation in athletics, and literary events helped off-set the emotional harshness of the school. They helped, but they didn't undo the emotional damage.

When toys or sports equipment was not available children "made do." "Cricket" was played with a book and a rolled up sock in the dorm after hours. Sometimes older students would sneak down from "Big End" to tell wild stories about pirates and tunnels.

When children were sick they went to "Iso," a wing in the small hospital at the upper end of the compound on the top floor. One December Kathy had Diphtheria. One of the teachers wrote Mac and Lillian that she could be heard singing at the top of her voice, " God Bless America", so apparently by that time her throat and her patriotism were both in good condition.

Students were taught to sing Scripture songs, which were composed by the leaders. Good thing. When the day came that their Bibles and song books were confiscated no one could take from them what they had stored in their heads and hearts. Here are several of the songs:

Anxious for nothing
Prayerful in everything

Thankful for anything
Peaceful through all

This is His promise sure
Made to the sons of men
Peace far beyond our ken
Guarding our thoughts.
(Phil 4: 6-7)

God is our Refuge
Our refuge and our strength
In trouble, in trouble
A very present help.

Therefore will not we fear
Therefore will not we fear
For the Lord of Hosts is with us
The Lord of Hosts is with us
The God of Jacob is our Refuge.

The Chefoo grace prayer was, "God is great and God is good; and we thank Him for our food; by His hand we all are fed, give us Lord our daily bread." Amen". The prayer for daily bread was more a predictor of the future than anyone could have imagined.

The use of "Prefects" was another feature of the British boarding school. Senior boys were selected for "leadership skills." They were used as stoolies for the administration and were, of course resented by other students.

Martha Philips, no relation to our family, was the only American teacher at the school and she was responsible to see that the American children met American educational standards. She would also accompany Richard and Kathy back to the U.S. More about THAT later.

School staff, both Chinese and foreigners, was given nicknames, i.e. "Goopy", for example. Foreign children born in China were assigned Chinese names at the time of their birth, and these names were registered at the Consulate, i.e. Kathy's name was Nai-Hua; Doris, Nai-Lian; Richard's Chinese name was Qing Hua. Information listing David's Chinese name has been lost. Our given family last name was Pei, to resemble our American name of Phillips.

"My times are in your hands."
Psalm 31:14 TLB

Life at Chefoo School had the rigidity and structure of a military camp, but life just outside the walls was becoming unglued.

"The Commander of the armies of heaven is here among us."
Psalm 46:7 TLB

CHAPTER 20

On February 3, 1938 the Japanese took over the city of Chefoo. The Chinese gave no resistance. It was a "peaceful take-over" according to the Japanese, but filled with less peace and more terror and tension for the locals.

Day after day truckloads of Japanese soldiers drove past the school. There was fighting on the other side of the hill from the school and students could hear the noise. The Japanese were un-loading sea planes with bombs on the beach in front of the school. One night the Japanese caught some Chinese trying to slip away disguised in sheepskins. They were shot.

At times massacres occurred outside the girls' sleeping quarters and staff members would take the girls down to the dining room for animated and very loud reading until the killing stopped.

Japanese language took the place of English in the Chinese schools' curriculum. The Chinese hated Japan and refused to buy Japanese goods, so the Japanese forced the purchase of their goods.

Japanese soldiers increasingly encroached on school life. Their baseball games took the place of students sporting events. Soldiers visit to the school increased. Bayonet practice with blood curdling shouts occurred daily, which terrified the younger children. And, children saw the atrocities and beatings of local Chinese.

The Japanese took over the use of the school property to show propaganda films to local Chinese. Japan promised freedom from "Western Imperialism" to the un-free subjects being forced to view the film. Both the Japanese army and their navy wanted the school buildings, so they finally erected a wall right down the middle of the school property so each military division could occupy half.

For eleven months the Japanese kept the school in constant turmoil. Teachers and staff did their best to keep the school going as usual, but soldiers and guards were in and out of classrooms all of the time. The noise of planes was nerve wracking. One of Chefoo's cooks was taken away and tortured. The war situation had become worse and worse. It was late 1941 and Kathy was 7 ½ and Richard was 12 years. David and Doris, still in the interior of China were 4 years old.

The CIM board sent word that missionaries who wanted to return to their home country could do so, but no one left. When Christmas vacation came in December 100 children who could travel home were secretly told to take all of their possessions. Two hundred children remained at the school, Richard and Kathy among them. Later two groups of students and staff were allowed to return to their home countries, but not Richard and Kathy. Some of these remaining children did not see their parents for 5 more years.

On December 8, 1941, following the bombing of Pearl Harbor, Japanese soldiers burst into the dining room where teachers and students sat and announced: "You are all prisoners of the Japanese military. Everything in this school belongs to us." They sat in silence too stunned to move or speak. Soldiers took all of the school's radios so news of the bombing was the last news report they heard until secret communication began.

All "foreign nationals" instantly became POWs. Seventeen British and American businessmen and staff, including the Headmaster of Chefoo were jailed, accused of being "foreign agents." They were released 17 days later.

Martha Philips, teacher, had to go across the city of Chefoo to the American Consulate to get citizenship papers for the American children in case they would be sent home. No one, including Martha was certain she would return to Chefoo alive.

Money for the school was confiscated so there was no money to buy food. God provided a businessman who needed to make a payment in the city where CIM was headquartered. The mission paid his bill and he paid the school in cash, which allowed the purchase of food.

Students, teachers and staff were issued armbands with the letter of their passport country. A for American, B for British, etc. and X for other "enemy nationals." Also, each child was to wear his Yellow Badge of National Shame, an attempt to force the school officials to support the, Glorious Emperor of the Rising Sun."

Families dug air raid shelters in their back yards. The noose was tightening. Children were told to pack and be ready to move at any moment. But where would they go? It was just as well that they did not know because it would not be good.

"For I know the one in whom I trust, and I am sure that he is able to safely guard all that I have given him until the day of his return."
2 Timothy 1:12 TLB

CHAPTER 21

Everything on the compound belonged to His Imperial Majesty; at least the soldiers thought so, and there was a notice nailed to the front gate that confirmed it. The soldiers believed that their ownership included food supplies in the kitchen. The staff was able to purchase enough food for the children to survive because of the "private banking arrangements" with businessmen, but there was not enough money to provide adequate nutrition for them and the diet was strict with everything rationed to ½ of the previous amount for each child including milk, bread, and eggs. There certainly was not enough food to feed the soldiers.

The youngest children were allowed 9 pieces of bread a day. They could eat one piece every five minutes at dinner. There was no fruit. If you liked cabbage and carrots, however, you were in luck. Children began losing weight and the staff gave them cod-liver oil, which helped prevent serious starvation.

The soldiers came regularly to the kitchen and demanded food. Wisely, the teachers made a legal-appearing form and told the Japanese they would be happy to supply the food items as long as they signed the paper. The food stealing stopped because the soldiers knew that what they were doing was illegal.

To save money the servants were dismissed and the children and teachers did the dishwashing, cleaning, laundry, and mending. Clothes were washed by hand on washboards. Coolies still came with their "honey-wagons" to dip out the toilet holding-tanks. The school well became contaminated because the soldiers did not use good hygiene, so all of the water had to be boiled.

The staff began ripping up scarves to make cardigans and wool stockings for the children in preparation for the bitter cold winter that was coming.

Early in the occupation children were allowed to send and receive one letter a month, but those letters did not always get through and before long no mail was allowed in or out. An innovative doctor who knew Mac and Lillian was allowed entrance to the compound to treat a Japanese soldier. He asked Richard and Kathy to write their names and a short sentence on a small piece of paper. He taped their messages on the inside of medicine bottles and then sent them to Gansu where they were received with tears and joy.

In August, the soldiers took over the hospital, doctor's house, and staff housing. In October, they demanded that the school vacate the building for the younger children and the children began sleeping in classrooms. There was no more school. One by one during the next weeks the Japanese took control of other buildings on the property and finally the school officials were told they had five days to be gone completely. The school was to become a military station.

The day of departure was November 5, 1942. Children were told to carry their bedside potties and march the two miles to their new home at Temple Hill, a deserted property of the Presbyterian Church. The youngest and the elderly rode in rickshaws and the other children and staff walked two by two, heads high and singing, "God is still on the throne, and He will remember His own..." The march through the streets was intended to humiliate the students and teachers but since the children did not understand the agenda they sang at the top of their lungs and marched with confidence, laughing and waving while hundreds of Chinese stood by the side of the road open-mouthed. The Japanese soldiers screamed orders for the crowd to spit, curse, and ridicule as the children marched but the orders were ignored. In addition to his potty, each child was allowed to carry his most precious item, his one lifeline to his family. It wasn't much, but it was something. In addition each student carried a cup, plate and a bowl along with utensils in a carrying bag which hung around his neck.

In the end, the Japanese carried away the children's personal books, textbooks and library books from the school to be used as waste paper.

Temple Hill Presbyterian Mission Compound was not the Hilton. It had been a family property with three houses plus some storage sheds in a rural area behind the city of Chefoo. On top of the hill was a Buddhist Temple where hundreds of people came to worship. Gongs and cymbals accompanied the chanting priests.

The first night 71 girls bedded down in an attic with beds for six. So much for needing privacy.

"He still rules from heaven. He closely watches everything that happens here on earth."
Psalm 11: 4 TLB

"For to you has been given the privilege not only of trusting him but also of suffering for him."
Philippians 1:29 TLB

"Your attitude should be the kind that was shown us by Jesus Christ, who, though he was God, did not demand and cling to his rights as God, but laid aside his mighty power and glory, taking the disguise of a slave and becoming like men."
Philippians 2:5 TLB

CHAPTER 22

As the children marched to their new concentration camp the Japanese soldiers took from them whatever they wanted. The children had so little, but were powerless to stop these angry men with guns. On arrival they found a small compound with walls of stone 12 feet high and 18 inches thick. The tops of the walls had pieces of broken glass embedded in them.

The soldiers said they should pile luggage outside of the houses and move in the next day. That night the staff went to check the gates and found that they had been greased and unlocked so the soldiers could return to steal that night. The staff men were no dummies and had brought padlocks of their own and locked the gates which kept the belongings safe.

It was cozy at Temple Hill. The 175 children slept in TWO houses each along with a few staff members. Older adults slept in the third house. The first night a herd of goats broke out of their enclosures and was ready to nibble on the pile of luggage. Fortunately one of the staff men had slept on top of the suitcases to prevent theft and midnight goat snacks.

The outside toilets lay flush to the ground in full public view with only an awning above. The smell was not good. A boy needed to jump from stone to stone until the final leap landed him on an island surrounded by maggots. He had then arrived at the "bathroom."

Water was scarce and had to be carried from the well. Richard's job, mixing coal dust into balls for cooking and heating, made getting washed at night with limited water was almost impossible. Each child washed in a small personal basin with his 2 inches of allotted water and then rinsed in a communal tub. Depending on your age, it was fun.

The staff had to buy their own food since the Japanese took no responsibility to supply it. Later some rations were provided when the Swiss Consul demanded that they do it, but not in the beginning. Teachers planted vegetables, and the goats did their part to provide milk. Chickens and a goose were added to the compound but the first batch of chickens drown in a basement flood and the goose suffered an early demise after he bit a teacher.

Chinese Christians on the other side of the wall found ways to drop food and occasional mail at night. But many Chinese were hungry and some were near starvation so thieves climbed over the wall at night, too, in search of food. Stealing from a prison camp of children was a last ditch effort to survive. Spies circulated outside the wall wearing long Chinese robes but with visible Japanese officer boots underneath. They were checking to see if there was any infraction of the rules or trading over the wall. There was, but not when the soldiers were looking.

The girls' house was approximately ½ mile from the boys' quarters. Richard and Kathy were allowed to visit two times a month. The staff and older students provided entertainment and music at night. Japanese officials gave permission for Sunday "Church" if an outline of the sermon was given to them two weeks before the target delivery date. Teachers and children prayed that some Japanese would come to faith in Christ after reading the sermon outlines. In keeping with the pattern at Chefoo School, devotions were held each morning and evening.

One 5 year old could not say "Concentration Camp". Instead, he said, "Consecration Camp", and he was right about that.

When the students and staff first arrived at Temple Hill there were no light bulbs, so two boys volunteered to ride their bikes back to Chefoo School and "liberate" some. Since the soldiers thought the school had been vacated, the mission was successful and they weren't caught.

At first there was no school, but the "vacation" didn't last long. All teaching materials and texts had been taken by the soldiers, so teachers taught from memory. There was no science equipment. Students sat on their beds for class. At the end of the war graduates were able to take the Oxford Entrance exams and there was not one failure.

Students were busy with studying and chores. It took hours of sitting on an oilcloth to peel potatoes for 200+ children and adults for one meal.

Two piglets were purchased and named, "Rudolph" and "Adolph" with the intent of fattening them for Christmas dinner. They grew rapidly, but two days before Christmas, "Rudolph became gravely ill." The children prayed and the adults administered some brandy and castor oil, and the pig recovered in time to be slaughtered. We are left wondering about the missionaries' access to the brandy.

Twice a day all of the students stood in line for roll call. An officer would yell, "Bango", which meant that it was time to number off. "Ichi, ni, san, shi", was sometimes substituted for, "Itchy knee, scratch a flea", and said fast enough the soldiers never questioned it.

In order to fill time, teachers began organizing Girl Scouts and Boy Scouts. Students learned to build and control fires, prepare and plan food for large numbers, and, to perform basic first aid. There was no merit badge for learning to eat tofu but there should have been and eating ground donkey was one of those things you were just better off not knowing about, badge or no badge. There was no fruit, rarely vegetables or meat, and no peanut butter.

Another batch of chickens was dropped over the wall but by the time they could be butchered, they had become "friends" of boys who had given each of them names. Fortunately just before the axe fell one chicken laid an egg and all of the chickens were placed on parole. Students were given an egg in alphabetical order, one a day as they became available. Calcium was supplied by pulverizing egg shells and giving a spoonful to each child.

The first morning at breakfast after they arrived, they heard the song, 'Standing on the Promises of God," played by a Chinese mission school band across the street. The boys had been forced into the Japanese army and used the song for marching practice. The words were unknown to the Japanese soldiers of course, but not to the musicians or their neighbors at Temple Hill.

The close sleeping arrangement helped keep everyone from freezing during the winter, but it was not an asset in the summer when the heat became unbearable. Some slept in a shed outside where the temperature during the day reached 116 degrees F, but still it was an improvement over sleeping in the house with 72 boys who had each bathed in two inches of water.

At Christmas teachers built a Christmas tree with branches nailed on. Children were asked to share one toy or make something to share with another child.

They owned almost nothing. It was another experience in letting go.

At the end of ten months at Temple Hill, rumors began to circulate that they would be moved to another prison camp. The location was 100 miles inland to the old walled city of Weihsien. There was no railroad between Chefoo and Weihsien so they would travel by boat and then train. It took two days for the journey. There were no toilets on board the ship and many of the children became sea sick. The only food that was provided was bread and some raw fish. There was nothing to drink. There were 300 of them on the tiny steamer so 100 students were jammed into the hold where they laid on the floor head to foot. It was smelly, but there were plenty of rats to distract them.

Finally they arrived and could see the high gray walls with the inscription, "The Courtyard of the Happy Way". The area was 150 by 200 yards with 60 run down, dilapidated, looted buildings, no running water and open cesspools for 1,800 prisoners. It didn't look good. They had been told "everything would be furnished" at Weishein so the Chefoo staff brought very little. Some of the earlier arrivals shared their sardine cans, a substitute for fine china to hold the meal allotments.

There were 3 kitchens and each of them prepared food for 700 prisoners or more. The food that was brought in was rotten when it arrived, but one day a bushel of apples came so each kitchen crew made apple pies to be shared with 700 mouths. If a prisoner didn't actually get his quota of one bite, at least he got a smell of a bite.

"The eternal God is your Refuge,
and underneath are the everlasting arms."
Deuteronomy 33:27 TLB

CHAPTER 23

The Courtyard of the Happy Way was none of the above. It was not a courtyard and there was nothing "happy" about it. Weihsien Alien Civilian Collection Center was another euphemism for this hellish concentration camp, but at least it didn't assume that it was a "happy" place.

In August of 1943 a list had been posted at Temple Hill of 56 students who would be repatriated to their home countries. Richard and Kathy's names were not on the list so they knew that they would be moved to Weihsien. They could not take photos or any handwritten material, including letters from parents. More and more the children were emotionally distanced from their parents. They were in a world that just did not include them.

The notice of transfer to Weihsien was sent to others in Shanghai who were to become POWs. The notice read, "For your safety and comfort…." some naïve adults assumed they were going to a luxurious country club and brought their golf clubs. Big mistake! Older women came in fur coats and elegant hats.

The Chefoo students would join the compound which was the size of a city block and they would live with Roman Catholic priests, monks, nuns, other missionaries, business men, university professors, prostitutes, and musicians. There were fifteen nationalities and eleven languages spoken among the POWs.

Successful business people had led pampered lives with servants, chauffeurs, and exclusive private schools for their children. Hand carved mahogany dining tables, glistening chandeliers, hunting rifles; first edition leather-bound books would be left behind and soon looted. Their houses would be sold on the black market. The women cried as they marched into camp.

There were multiple nationalities here and the only thing they had in common was that the Japanese did not want them roaming freely around China.

Six-foot walls surrounded the camp. Guard towers with soldiers with machine guns were in each corner and electrified wire ran across the top of the walls. The property had previously been owned by the Presbyterian Church and contained a hospital, chapel, and, school buildings. That was a long time ago and now it wouldn't qualify as inhabitable. There was no furniture in the buildings, and the floors were damp.

The six over-flowing toilets were 150 yards from the center field where prisoners were counted off each day. None of the toilets flushed and no one wanted to wade into the excrement to haul off the feces. Finally some nuns, priests and missionaries put scarves on their noses and did the job. In the end, they were able to flush with ½ bucket of water after each use.

Prisoners scrounged through piles of rubbish for usable items to "furnish" their rooms.

Chefoo students and staff arrived at the camp after it had been functioning for 1 ½ years. There were 2,000 prisoners by then. It was August 1943.

Rain turned the compound into a mud swamp, but that was the least of the weather concerns since winter weather was like Chicago but without indoor heating. Children continued to grow and clothing was made from curtains and blankets salvaged from Chefoo School. Prisoners washed their hands in ice water dripping from faucets. The Japanese soldiers ordered everyone to turn in their cash "for safe keeping." Most people hid their money in their underwear, a much safer place than in the care of the Japanese.

One of the earliest priorities was setting up a working hospital. There were excellent surgeons and other doctors interned at Weihsien, but they had no medicines and no equipment to treat patients. Patients with contagious diseases were housed in the morgue, including a Catholic nun and a 12-year old girl. When the nun died the girl was left alone with the bodies of those who had recently died.

For meals a 70-yard line of quiet, grim emaciated people stood to wait for a thin watery soup and a slice of bread. Same Old Stew (SOS), a mixture of eggplant and chopped weeds picked from around camp with some water added was dinner. It was a grayish glob, the kind of thing you would never eat unless you were starving. Breakfast was porridge without milk and some more bread. A third of the prisoners at camp were children. When their teeth started to come in without enamel, egg shells were ground up and given to them.

There was a thriving black market at camp with farmers outside the wall offering eggs and vegetables for those with money. The Red Cross sent occasional packages for prisoners of the United States. And, food could be purchased at the canteen, again only for those with money, which did not include Richard or Kathy.

In "The Three Penny Opera," Bertolt Brecht wrote, "Even saintly folk will act like sinners unless they have their customary dinners." It was true. People were starving and desperate. The Japanese siphoned off most of the rations for the camp and prisoners were either malnourished or starving. The final eight weeks before the Japanese surrendered there was almost no food except bread for the camp.

Why didn't teachers or students escape? Because individually they could not wander undetected in

China and Chinese were rewarded well for information leading to their capture. Two men DID escape in the first few days and sent updates on the war secretly to camp. They were heroes and very, very lucky.

The Red Cross also arranged for letters to go out, 25 spaces in all, but it took 6 months to reach the recipient, and another 6 months for a return letter. E-mail was not an option.

Everyone was required to do three hours a day of manual labor, including the children. All empty cans were reshaped to make bricks from coal dust.

Life was grim at Weihsien, but the worst was yet to come.

"Hide your loved ones in the shelter of your presence, safe beneath your hand, safe from all conspiring men. Blessed is the Lord for he has shown me that his never failing love protects me like the walls of a fort."
Psalm 31: 20-21 TLB

CHAPTER 24

Three hundred monks at Weihsien Concentration Camp were housed next to the wall. They managed to pry a few bricks loose from an obscure corner where the lights from the guard tower did not shine. Chinese farmers on the other side of the wall were eager to claim the Red Cross "comfort" money received by the POWs in exchange for eggs, so cash was quietly slipped through the hole and eggs began to flow.

If a guard approached Father Darby, the "look out" monk, Father Scanlon, would begin a loud Gregorian chant and Father Darby would cover the eggs with his long brown robe and begin to pray LOUDLY. The guards were afraid of these "holy men," so usually moved on quickly. At the height of the egg smuggling business, two-thirds of the prisoners had an egg each day, approximately 1,300 eggs traveled through the hole in the wall with the shells providing needed calcium for children.

One day a guard lifted Father Darby's robe and found 150 eggs in his lap. The guard was sure that being a "holy man" didn't equip him to lay eggs, so he was hauled off to "solitary confinement" for six weeks. It was a punishment that brought gales of laughter to the packed crowd at the "trial." Father Darby had spent 25 years in a Trappist monastery with a vow of silence prior to his capture. Six more weeks would not be a problem!

Later, when a Chinese farmer tried to climb over the wall to deliver food, he was electrocuted and his body was allowed to remain on the wire as a gruesome warning. The egg smuggling ended, but for one full year God had taken care of his children by supplying them with the eggs they desperately needed.

There were a variety of contests in camp, many of them athletic competitions. The monks had the best baseball team. But other contests occurred too. The medical staff sponsored "rat catching" contests. The record catch for one day was 68 rats. Chefoo students initiated their own "fly catching" contests and 50 were caught during one church service, during a sermon on the plagues, most likely.

In camp former status, money, education, and family connections were totally irrelevant. What did matter was integrity. Food parcels were delivered to the 200 Americans in the camp containing special food items. They each received several parcels but they were not willing to share with the other starving prisoners. The Japanese soldiers forced the Americans to share so that every prisoner would receive one parcel. Did the term "ugly American" originate at Weihsien?

Workers were assigned to the kitchen based on their moral character and reputation for not stealing food. Some prisoners lost 100 lbs. during the duration of incarceration. Most adults lost 50 to 75 lbs.

Some prisoners sewed large pockets in the lining of their coats and stole extra potatoes in the food line. One man was caught with 15 potatoes. But discipline was a problem. To send someone to "jail" where he would be alone, away from annoying neighbors, have time to read, and avoid his work duty was coveted. There were 18 inches between a prisoner's bed and the person next to him and it was in these 18 inches that he must use his chamber pot. Going to jail would be a good thing; yes, please.

Medicines for the hospital were brought in creatively. A form with a typed list of all of the drugs from local pharmacies was entered on every other line. Then the required officer signature was obtained. After that the antibiotics and other hard to find drugs which were secretly provided by Chinese Christians were entered on the alternate lines. With the official signature already in place the forms were never questioned.

Eric Liddell, of *Chariots of Fire* fame, winner of the gold medal in the 1924 Olympics was a POW at Weihsien. All Christians and non-Christians, adults and children who knew him as "Uncle Eric" loved him. His work assignment was to teach math and science three hours a day to children and to organize activities for them. He sold the gold watch he earned as an Olympic medal winner in order to buy supplies for the children. He supervised hockey games, ran a Friday night youth group with square dancing, quiz shows, chess tournaments, and more. Richard and Kathy knew him as their beloved teacher and friend.

Eric died just a few weeks before the end of the war from a brain tumor. His funeral was packed out. His chosen song, "I Know That My Redeemer Lives," was sung at his service as well as the Scripture verse that was associated with his life, I Samuel 2:30 (TLB), "Them that honor me I will honor."

Sanitation in the camp was a nightmare. Open cesspools were next to the sleeping rooms of children. The stench hung over the eating area. Gangs of Chinese coolies with buckets at each end of a pole carried the "night soil" to fields outside of the camp every day.

For a while tying money to a brick with a letter attached and throwing it over the wall was the primary means of "airmail" to get messages out of camp. An ingenious prisoner found a list of Chinese names and addresses in the abandoned hospital on the property and these were used as "return addresses" thereby avoiding post office suspicion. But when an additional barbed wire fence was installed on top of the wall, it became impossible to launch a brick over it. A new plan was needed.

One of the missionaries volunteered to assist the coolies in removing the latrine contents and since there was little competition for the position, he was readily appointed as the "Sanitary Patrol Captain." His first task was to build a small leak-proof metal box into which he placed the precious letters of children to their parents. He placed the box in the bucket and then filled the bucket with its odiferous haul. The chance of inspection of the buckets was slim to none. Outside, Chinese Christians retrieved the box and sent the letters on their way. During the years at Weihsien, Mac and Lillian received one letter from Richard and Kathy.

Later cesspool mail delivery became too risky and another method of delivering mail had to be found. Again, the ingenious "Sanitary Patrol Captain" observed that the mail brought in to the Japanese officers arrived each week by a bicycle carrier. The mailman was searched on arrival and then was escorted into the guard house where the mail bag was opened. An empty second bag was left at the bicycle. During this brief absence, the former SPC quickly placed a packet of letters with an American dollar on top and then ran to hide in the bushes. When the mailman observed the new addition the SPC peeked out of his hiding spot and smiled broadly. The mailman nodded in return and the mail of Weihsien Concentration Camp began to flow again.

One important letter needed to be sent to the American Embassy asking for medication and money to purchase food which could then be smuggled into camp. It was a dangerous letter to send, so it was

125

written on silk and then sewed inside the soles of cloth shoes before smuggling the shoes out of camp. The letter arrived at the Embassy and the needed money and medicines arrived.

The day came that Richard and Kathy's names were posted for exchange with Japanese POW's and they left Weihsien accompanied by Martha Philips, one of the teachers, for the journey home. Their stay at Weihsien had been shorter than many of the prisoners, but it left its mark.

The trip home would not be easy. Some trips are easier than others. This one would be a nightmare.

"You were there while I was being formed in utter seclusion. You saw me before I was born and scheduled each day of my life before I began to breathe. Every day was recorded in your book."
Psalm 139:15 TLB

CHAPTER 24

Leaving Weihsien in the fall of 1943 brought a mix of feelings including excitement, relief, and sadness at the loss of friends who Richard and Kathy would never see again, as well as some fear for their unknown future. They were on their way to see their parents, who they knew a little, and their twin siblings who they hardly knew at all, in a strange new country. They were going "home" except that China was the only home they knew. Richard was 13 and Kathy was 10 years old. Mac and Lillian, Dave and Doris were still in the interior of China.

There were 25 Chefoo students who would be exchanged for Japanese POWs. In the beginning the Japanese had demanded five Japanese for every American, but that ploy didn't work. It would be 1:1. The rest of the prisoners would be held at Weihsien until the end of the war in 1945, three years later.

Martha Philips was one of the adults assigned to deliver this precious cargo out of China to the U.S. The trip inland was supposed to take two days to reach Shanghai but the Japanese anticipated bombings along the way, so the train took the long way to avoid harm to the POWs because each one was worth one Japanese life. They were crammed into train coaches designed for 60 people. There were 300 in the 3 cars, but then they were accustomed to tight quarters.

They arrived at St. John's University in Shanghai for their first meal in four days. It was stew and bread.

Finally they boarded an old French ship, the Teia Maru, which had a normal capacity of 400 passengers and now had 1600 POWs packed in. The ship was a dirty, smelly freighter which began the trip in Kobe, Japan. It was definitely a slow boat to China.

Large white crosses protected the Teia Maru from Allied subs and planes and they identified the ship as on a humanitarian mission. In the evening children and missionaries gathered on the deck in the light of the crosses to sing hymns.

Sleeping quarters for the women and girls were on the main deck on straw ticks (mattresses filled with grass and weeds). The ticks were lumpy, 6 feet long and 15-24 inches wide, but at this point no one was fat. There were 35 lined up in a row with another shelf 18 inches above them, so 240 ticks in one small space. Kathy had 127 roommates in her section. The men and boys were worse off and slept in the hold of the ship where there was less circulation and more odors.

On deck there were 100 chairs for the 1600 people. Drinking water was provided 2X day for a period of 30 minutes, except when the crew forgot to provide it. Flies were dense. The bathrooms were filthy. The putrid odor from the lower decks where Richard had to sleep was bad. There was no laundry for the month long trip home. Richard's clothes had been stolen from his trunk so he didn't have much need for laundry, anyway.

The same glasses were used for each seating in the dining room…three group seatings for each meal. Each glass was filled with 3 inches of water. If a passenger drank part of the water it was refilled to the 3 inch line for the next person. The glasses were not washed between seatings.

Meals consisted of rice and worms, rotten eggs, boiled cabbage, and some spoiled dry fish. They could take or leave it, but there was no other food and weevils, worms and other insects were the only fresh meat available. Martin Luther's, "Diet of Worms," was the menu here. There was a shortage of bread, but some passengers had money and could buy a slice for $5.00. Martha bought a loaf each day to feed the students.

Five hundred passengers had dysentery. No surprise considering the sanitation, or in this case, the LACK of it. When they arrived in New York one reporter wrote that this was "the most emaciated group of Americans he had ever seen." As a weight loss program-it was highly effective.

Someone has written that when you are a little hungry you talk about food. When you are VERY hungry you don't talk but you THINK about food. When you are starving you neither talk nor think about food. Richard and Kathy didn't talk or think about it. They were on the Teia Maru for 35 days.

More Americans were added from a Philippine internment camp. The ship stopped at Goa, India for the exchange of Japanese prisoners who would board the Teia Maru and the Chefoo group along with the other POWs would board the beautiful Swedish liner, The Gripsholm. It was October 15.

A Japanese POW had committed suicide en route to the prisoner exchange so the 1:1 exchange of prisoners was un-even. One of the missionaries volunteered to return to Weihsien and the Japanese were startled by this gesture and eventually agreed to allow all of the Americans to be sent home even though the exchange was un-even.

The Gripsholm was partly staffed by volunteer Americans from the US who had chosen to bring these POW's home. One of them began singing, *"America, The Beautiful."* It was a song that the children had never heard. Hum a few bars of the British national anthem and they'd join right in.

The Chefoo group remained on the Teia Maru for three days while the Red Cross stowed food and clothing on the ship. Someone on the Gripsholm called out asking what they were hungry for and began throwing fruit to the deck of the Teia Maru. Some of it fell into the ocean, which was painful. They were SO hungry.

The Japanese coming off of the Gripsholm were wearing beautiful clothing and carried handsome luggage. They looked like tourists. They were going to be in for a shock!

The Gripsholm was roomy, luxurious and incredibly clean. Cabins with two berths became cabins for four, which was the most sleeping space Richard and Kathy had ever remembered.

A small group of Christians among the Japanese POWs who gathered at the edge of the deck along with students from Chefoo began to sing, "Jesus shall reign where 'ere the sun doth his successive journeys run." And then, "In Christ there is no East or West."

One year later after the Teia Maru again became a transport ship it was hit by torpedoes and sank in 20 minutes.

The Gripsholm was a floating palace. As they boarded, a Red Cross lady handed the children the largest chocolate bar each child had ever seen. The children who could not resist ate it and promptly vomited.

The first noon meal was beyond imagination, more like a hallucination. In the dining room was spread a massive smorgasbord with every delicious fresh fruit and delicacy known to man (and starving child).

Overnight clothing was returned to each cabin fresh and crisply starched and folded. The Red Cross provided new clothes for the children who had long ago outgrown their school uniforms and the make-do outfits made from curtains. Richard finally could change clothes.

There were several stops along the way, one of them at Port Elizabeth where they were treated like royalty. All food at restaurants was free. At Rio de Janeiro they were taken to the top of Sugar Loaf Mountain.

A team of doctors examined each child for communicable diseases and a diplomatic service worker ensured that each one would be met at the harbor in NY. Richard had memorized the address of Uncle Kenneth's house in Portland. His good memory didn't surprise anyone.

Many of the children had letters waiting, the first in two years for some. The newspapers had published a list of those being exchanged so families could meet the ship in NY and also so that they could send letters to the ship.

Lee and Minera Hurst, Lillian's parents who lived in Albany, OR would meet the ship in NY but did not have permission to take the children home.

After two weeks on the Atlantic the ship entered the mouth of the Hudson River and someone called, "There she is, the Statue of Liberty!" It was a foggy December day and Lady Liberty was shrouded in fog, but the prospect of freedom was clearly in sight.

After 75 days on the sea at approximately 10 a.m., they docked at Pier F and were met by the CIM mission staff and taken to the Philadelphia headquarters, a spacious house in the Germantown district of Philadelphia. The children would remain there and attend local schools for three months until their parents returned to the US.

A part of the welcome home was a party given by New York Girl Scout Troop # 126 for the Chefoo Girl Scouts where each Chefoo girl was given Christmas gifts and together they sang Christmas carols.

Back in China Mac and Lillian were notified that their children had arrived safely in the US and they began the journey to join them. Mac said later that the most expensive part of their trip was the travel by donkey since they needed to pay for the donkey as well as a man to walk beside him an "encourage" the animal to move.

After Mac and Lillian and the twins arrived via ship in Los Angeles they flew to Oregon. The CIM staff was notified and Martha Philips, who lived in the northwest agreed to transport Richard and Kathy on the final lap of the journey to Albany. Just before the scheduled departure date Kathy came down with mumps and the trip was delayed.

While they were at the CIM headquarters Richard and Kathy went to a nearby store to buy washcloths. They spoke with a strong British accent and asked the clerk for "flannels," British terminology, but when they were not understood they ran back to the Mission in embarrassment. It wouldn't be the last time their British accents would create a problem.

Being reunited with family in March 1944 was an adjustment. Did Richard and Kathy call their parents Mother and Father, or the British Mummy and Daddy? And, then there would be the adjustment to public schools and the questions about prison camps by reporters. Kathy learned to say, "I forgot."

There was drama ahead for the remaining POWs at Weihsien Concentration Camp. For now the war continued.

> "He brings them safely into harbor."
> Psalm 107:30 TLB

CHAPTER 26

Eric Liddell, the loved "flying Scotsman" and Olympic gold medalist died in February of 1945, six months before the Weihsien Camp was closed. Word had leaked out that the Japanese planned to "liquidate" the POWs there, and the U.S. made immediate plans to rescue the prisoners.

Prisoners were tired of freezing winters, ragged clothing, and bed bugs in the summer and rats year around. They were tired of cesspools, tired of the hard work to keep the camp going, and tired of trying to keep the peace with irritable neighbors. They were emaciated and beyond hunger.

It was August of 1945 when the first sound of a B24 plane labeled, "The Armored Angel," was heard overhead. The door opened and seven paratroopers jumped with parachutes. They landed prepared to fight, but instead the GI's were smothered with kisses and picked up and carried around on the suddenly empowered shoulders of prisoners. One paratrooper was a former Chefoo student!

The new arrivals were taken to the Japanese Chief military officer, Major Kosaka, and he quietly laid his samurai sword and gun on the table in front of the American officer.

The Armored Angel left, but every four days eleven B29s circled the camp and dropped huge cases of food, clothes, and magazines. Eating cans of tomato soup after a diet of near starvation made the children sick. They had survived on less and less bread in the months before the end of the war. Amazingly, no one was injured by the "bombs" of cans!

One prisoner ate the shaving cream; another swallowed an entire bottle of vitamins. Good judgment about what to eat went out a long time ago. The newly popular song, "Don't Fence Me In," blared from the radio. In early October a troop ship arrived to take the Americans home. They would be 4 ½ weeks at sea and dock in San Francisco. Initially the sick and elderly and children were shipped out, followed by families and finally singles. The war was over.

POWs were going home to make huge adjustments. At Chefoo they had no money, no phone, no busses, no shops, no dogs, and very little soap. They would be overwhelmed to find aisles of cereal boxes, canned vegetables, fresh meat, and more fruit than even their dreams could accommodate. Kathy was in Oregon and had already discovered blueberries.

"God is able to make it up to you by giving you everything you need and more, so that there will not only be enough for your own needs, but plenty left over to give joyfully to others."
2 Corinthians 9:8 TLB

CHAPTER 27

Seventy-three years after Malcolm and Lillian Phillips went to China, their adult children Richard, Kathy, Dave, and Doris returned to retrace their early beginnings, accompanied by Lillian, Richard's wife and Marilyn, Dave's wife. A local Chinese travel guide looked at our itinerary and remarked, "NO ONE wants to go THERE." He was wrong. We did want to go there.

We visited four Provinces and traveled by plane, train, bus, and by foot. The only missing means of transportation was donkey, and we actually didn't miss that at all. We found the site where Dave and Doris were born at Fenyang, we visited the concentration camp at Temple Hill and saw the room where Richard slept with 72 of his closest friends, we visited Eric Liddle's grave. We visited the town where Kathy was born which was the first city of ministry by our parents. We walked the beach where Chefoo School once stood. We worshipped in thriving Chinese churches that our Father had founded.

We met elderly Christians who had come to faith in Christ through our father's ministry. When I commented to our Chinese guide about how gracious and kind the people were to us he replied, "Oh, it's not YOU. It is your parents that they honor." Of course.

One elderly man told us that his brother was executed because our Father had spent hours teaching him English. He was a good student and became fluent, but was killed because his English was too good. It was apparent he had spent time with our Father.

At one church Richard spoke and our communist guide, not a Christian, interpreted for him. We loved watching that happen. God must have smiled.

Some experiences were just funny. "You are fatter than your Mother," or "Your nose isn't as long as hers."

At one of our father's churches a brass band composed of church members in white and red uniforms formed two long lines outside the church and played as we got off the bus and headed into the church. Afterwards we were served potatoes.

Some of the Christians who knew us as children were shocked to learn the story of how we had made it out of China alive during the Japanese invasion. They had risked their lives to save ours during our parent's ministry. At one tiny church we stood in a circle and sang The Lord's Prayer, them in Chinese and us in English. It was the worst possible music because we were all crying, yet it was the music of heaven.

When one of our tour guides shared that she had difficulty with an adequate supply of breast milk for her baby I suggested that she drink more water. She later said that she had started eating pig's feet and her milk supply was just fine now. Why didn't I think of that?

The babies in the rural areas did not wear diapers. Their little bare bottoms hung out from the slit in their pants and moms took them to the side of the road as needed. I commented that American babies all wear diapers and the Chinese mom looked at me blankly and asked, "Don't they KNOW when their baby needs to go?" The answer is, "no."

We visited a Bible School, which charged $18 a month for room, board, and tuition. They slept seven to a bed which minimized the need for linens and maximized fellowship.

Managing squat potties (a hole on the floor) on a jerking, moving train was interesting, not to mention sharing the same bathroom with both men and women.

Restaurants offered a variety of food choices: Stir Fried Intestines, Live Snake in Plum Sauce, Tendons in Chili Oil, and Marinated Duck Tongue. We ate scrambled eggs with chopped tomatoes. No mystery ingredients.

We visited the Anglican Union Church where Richard and Kathy had attended on Sundays when they were students at Chefoo. We got the last seats in the balcony of the 1,000 member church where 300 new believers were baptized the previous year. One of the songs that morning was, "God Will Take Care of You." It was hard to sing and cry at the same time.

Thomas Wolfe once wrote, "You can't go home again." And, it was a different China than the place of our childhood, but the heart-tie to Gansu was strong and we all knew that in some way we were "home". There will be more time to talk in heaven and we'll remember our earlier Chinese language skills then.

"Be not dismayed what e'er betide,
God will take care of you
Beneath His wings of love abide,
God will take care of you."
"Thru days of toil when heart doth fail,
God will take care of you,
When dangers fierce your path assail,
God will take care of you."
-Civilla Martin

CHAPTER 28

Gordon and Kathy Fairley arrived in Kinshasa (Leopoldville) in 1961 with 5-year-old Sharon, 3-year-old Donny, and baby Darlene who was 1 year. Gordon would be flying "routine missions" for Missionary Aviation Fellowship (MAF) and the family would live in a house on the property of the Baptist Mission Station. "Routine" life didn't last long until all hell broke loose and "routine" evaporated. For the next three years the family would live and work in the middle of a revolution.

The family had stopped in Geneva for language school on their way to Congo in order to learn French, although Gordon already spoke French from his growing up years in Gabon, and Darlene wasn't speaking much at all. They would all learn to speak Lingala after they arrived in Congo.

Gordon was excited to fly his small aircraft as a bush pilot and serve Christ at the same time. His parents remained "next door" in Gabon, although he would see them only one time during his 15-year Congo service. The rest of the family was excited to begin their new life in Africa even though it included eating crocodile, which they were told, "Tasted like fish," and fried caterpillars, a delicacy in Congo which tasted like caterpillars.

Bush flying was nasty business. No one was more aware of this than the seasoned pilots with MAF who compiled records of snatching folks from dangerous situations throughout Congo, even when the country was peaceful and the flights were "routine."

Gordon and Kathy were not trying to be heroic. Years before they had settled the matter of, "by life or by death" and they knew that although someone might kill their bodies, they couldn't kill their souls. They knew that the safest place to be was wherever God had placed them.

Congo was big, the third largest country in Africa with 910 square miles, 15 million people in multiple tribes with hundreds of languages. African languages are complex and have been described as on par with learning Latin. There were no words to explain the Christian message.

Many of its people had some primitive ideas about life and death. Eating the brain of a great Chief could provide needed medicine. Cannibalism transmitted the qualities of the person who was killed to the one eating him. Captured victims were forced to drink poison. Fetishes were used to ward off the evil spirits. The white man was a bleached out ghost that lived under the ocean. He came on ships that rose out of the water as they crossed the horizon. Polygamy included child marriage and infanticide. Large shares of the women were assigned to the older and wealthier men.

Congolese people were intelligent, but uninformed due to lack of education, belief in witchcraft, and primitive magical religious practices. The people were completely illiterate, unable to read or write, so new ideas did not spread easily. Paternalism in the writings of older missionaries described them as "savages." Colonialism used and abused Congolese to "keep them in their place" evaluating African culture through a Western lens. One annoyance to Western businessmen working in Africa was finding that Africans were seldom punctual and frequently did not bother to keep appointments at all.

The equator runs through the country giving it an average temperature of 77 degrees F, but with some snowcapped mountains. It was one of the riches countries in all of Africa with surpluses of palm oil products, rubber, coffee, bananas, diamonds, tea and cotton, just the kind of place that white men wanted to control.

King Leopold of Belgium took over Congo in 1877 and Belgium built roads, railroads, bridges, and provided medical services, but in time, most Congolese began to resent their rulers and wanted to be free from the yoke of white rule. Traders had been treated unfairly and atrocities were committed.

Negro slaves had gone to numerous European settlements along the coast of Africa. The slave trade was a curse that lasted 300 years and drained its population. Domestic slavery occurred too, and Chiefs were buried with hundreds of slaves to provide attendants in the spirit world.

Africa had no deep bays indenting its coasts and navigation on its rivers was stopped less than 100 miles from the mouth of the Congo River by rocks and rapids. The country was almost completely land-locked. In time railroads were built and airstrips made the interior more accessible.

Historically, central Africa became known as the "white man's grave." A third of the missionaries sent to Congo died within a space of weeks or months. The longest survivors lasted two years. Most of those early missionaries were in their 20s, but stamina and vitality could not resist the deadly tropical diseases. Life span was longer now, but jungle disease was as much a death threat as jungle natives. Gordon and Kathy, Sharon, Donny and Darlene would live in Congo for 15 years.

The Congo jungle was vivid and intense and a canopy of foliage so dense that when a tree died it rarely fell. It remained propped up for years by its neighbors. Wild orchids bloomed in profusion. Brilliant birds flitted through thickets. Monkeys screeched as they leaped overhead.

Occasionally an elephant barged through the undergrowth like a bulldozer. The rivers and streams were filled with crocodiles waiting patiently with only their eyes above water for the moment to murder.

Deadly brown and yellow pythons, some of them 20 feet long glided thought stagnant pools, which were home to swarms of mosquitoes, fatal fevers waiting to happen.

On June 30, 1960, only months after Gordon and Kathy arrived with their family in Leopoldville, Congo would be granted independence from Belgium. Unbelievable chaos would soon follow.

"For even before I was born God had chosen me to be His, and called me."
Galatians 1:15 TLB

CHAPTER 29

The revolution in Congo did not happen overnight. Since Congo had been declared independent by Belgium there had been a growing sense of discontent. Politicians had promised that their people would be promoted to positions of authority and wealth just like their previous white leaders. It sounded good, except that no Congolese had reached a rank above Sergeant in the Army and on the first day of independence, Sergeants became Generals. Secretaries became managers. They had no idea what do to in their new roles. For months after independence Congo had no functioning government.

The new Congolese leaders, intoxicated with power promised that there would be no more taxes, no more hard labor in the fields for the women, there would be secondary schools in every village, along with paved roads, large homes, bicycles, cars, and an abundance of food and clothes for all. Dead ancestors would be raised to life and would bring truckloads of money. Women were ordered to clear wide paths to the village graveyards so that the resurrected with all of their riches could drive to their village homes unhindered. Kathy said that some Congolese thought "independence" would come on a train!

In less than a year the reality of independence had become a bitter, distressing disappointment. Instead of the promised Utopia there was economic collapse, inter-tribal warfare, unemployment, graft, bribery, an undisciplined army and a very unstable government.

People began to ask when independence would end. Or, they suggested giving "independence" back to Belgium. When they realized it didn't work that way and they were on their own to solve these problems, people responded with helpless resignation. The average Congolese harbored intense bitterness toward Europeans believing that they had taken their autonomy. They were right about that.

There had been no transition, no training, and no sharing of information to support the new Congolese leadership. Belgium pulled out within two weeks of announcing their scheduled departure, and within a matter of days after that Congo was beginning to fall apart. Tribal groups took over the country, which was rapidly moving toward chaos. Congo called on the United Nations to help, and the UN sent a peacekeeping force but there was no peace to be kept and on June 30 the UN pulled out when the money to pay them was gone.

Cloth, matches, salt, soap and other necessities of life were becoming hard to get. The stage was set for a rebel take-over.

Congolese leaders began training in Peking (Beijing) where they were indoctrinated and trained in the art of guerrilla warfare. They were told that one arrow would kill nine men. Each soldier would receive an injection of "anti-bullet serum," and, if they were shot, the bullet would turn to water and cause no harm. Some leaders were trained at secret camps in the forest. They greeted each other as, "Comrade."

Many of the soldiers were 9-10 year olds and some of them had attended mission schools. When Bibles became available it was the Simbas who purchased them. They didn't understand what was happening and they thought they were fighting for their country's good. Naked children with their parasite loaded protruding tummies, their white shiny teeth strong from a diet of calcium loaded bugs and worms were ready to begin the reign of terror with spears, arrows and clubs and eventually these children would be given Tommy guns and automatic weapons. At times bare-chested rebels walked into a village without weapons, but waving palm branches and the villagers fled in sheer terror.

Other rebels included half naked, drug crazed young men whipped into frenzy. Smoking hemp before an attack provided artificial courage. Many soldiers were not in sympathy with the rebellion but were forced to go along with it if they wanted to live.

The first task on the agenda was to kill white people. Get rid of them. White business people fled to mission stations and were dragged out for torture. Young white schoolgirls as well as nuns were carried into the forest, raped and left naked. Some jeunesse (youth) were assigned to distribute literature, which no one could read.

There were rules for the soldiers: The blood of victims was to be smeared on their bodies. To wash it off would destroy its power to nullify the bullets and weapons of the enemy. To touch a white person or a woman would also destroy the magic power of the blood. When receiving items from whites they had to be placed on the ground so they could be taken without touching the white person. If they received a mortal wound it was apparent that they had not obeyed the rules, however after three days they would be resurrected to continue the fight. No stealing, no adultery, no drunkenness, and face straight ahead when going into battle. Never step in the blood of a fallen rebel. Hate grew stronger and there was no rule against hatred.

Most rebels reverted to age-old practices of witchcraft and cannibalism, as well. They would make fetishes out of the hearts of Americans and Belgians. The role of the witch doctor was to prepare concoctions of herbs and animal hearts to make the soldiers "bullet proof" when it was rubbed on their bodies. At the recruitment ceremony young rebels were told to turn their back and walk away. A gunshot was fired straight up into the air and the Simba was told he was immune to bullets. When you are nine years old, you believe that kind of thing.

The rebels would send young soldiers into a village shouting, "SIMBA (the Swahili word for "Lions") are coming." Then the Simbas would terrorize the village with their bows and arrows and if someone objected to joining their army, they were killed on the spot. The Simbas were uninformed about the idea of voluntary enlistment.

Simbas wore grass skirts and feathers and hats with leopard skin. Monkey or rhino were acceptable substitutes if leopard skin was not available. Goat horns protruded from their hats. Fetish bags containing mysterious witch doctor powder hung around their necks. Some Simbas had bits of military uniforms; many wore stolen ladies panties over their shorts. On their heads they wore cowboy hats, lampshades, or steel helmets. They were not allowed to fight in the rain, so there was no need for umbrellas. Night came suddenly in Congo due to its proximity to the equator, so by 6:30 p.m. the rebels retreated to their camps.

These "Leopard men" attached steel claws to their fingers and then howled like an animal they raked their victims to death.

Cutting the forehead of the rebel was a part of preparation for battle as was a daily baptism in which "dawa" would make bullets turn to water. A sorcerer or a commanding officer performed the ritual and then narcotics were rubbed into the cuts, which made these young soldiers wild and willing to run into enemy fire.

It didn't matter what service the white person provided to the Congolese, all that mattered was that he was white. First the rebels would conquer Leopoldville, then Brussels and then on to New York. "Someday the world will be ours!" they shouted and they believed it. The radio incited intense hatred for

Americans: "Congo has been sold to Americans and we have become their slaves. Fight to free our land."

No trains were running. No boats moving. Telegraph wires had been cut. Roads were blocked. Teachers and road workers had not been paid for a year.

Men, women, and children were forced to run at the command of rebels. Missionaries who defied the attempts of the rebels to force them to smoke hemp were beaten, tied and flung on live anthills. Gordon and Kathy understood the hours of agony for missionaries that resulted from being eaten by Congo termites. Dying men were forced to watch as their own bowels were eviscerated and eaten by rebels.

Idle young men, disillusioned by independence that didn't make them healthy, wealthy, or wise, robbed, pillaged, destroyed, threatened, tortured, and killed off intellectuals who were obviously "American agents." The people they killed had irreplaceable administrative skills and experience.

Mr. Patrice Lumumba formed the National Congolese Movement, which won widespread support in northeast Congo, but rebel forces soon assassinated him. The prestige of Lumumba was not derived from his educational background, which was only grade school, or in his character since he was arrested for embezzling $2,200 and spent two years in jail. It was his remarkable charismatic personality that charmed the masses.

Statues to Lumumba were erected in all large cities and following his death many of the executions were performed in front of Lumumba monuments and done with grotesque cruelty, including disembowelment of still living victims and consumption of various body parts. Sharon said that the blood stained sidewalks at Lumumba monuments became permanently red. No rain could wash away the stain.

Following a massacre Simbas attended local church services and joined in singing Christian hymns. The fight was about nationality and race, not faith.

The people they came to serve were stalking white missionaries throughout Congo. Some had already been executed and others were in hiding waiting in the jungle for the sound of the MAF plane. Gordon was their life-line to escape. "Routine" mission flights were definitely over. Gordon was in the right place at the right time for the right reason.

"Loving God means doing what he tells us to do."
I John 5:3 TLB

CHAPTER 30

"Oh! For the joy when worlds now wrecked with sin,
No more shall shed the life blood of our kin,
When God and saints, one family complete,
Shall know the names of those
Who laid their lives at His dear feet."
-Leonard Harris

Lumumba had promised that at independence the people would all turn white, become rich, live in big houses just like the Europeans, drive fancy cars, and no one would have to work. Some believed that Lumumba would return to earth in a "second coming" to fulfill his promises.

Congo was totally unprepared for independence. There were 30 university graduates in the 14 million people. Transition from one form of government to another generally takes 10-15 years, not two weeks.

In the past a Congolese who got a job started wearing a tie, a symbol that he had arrived. Since the rebel invasion no one dared to wear a tie because it identified him as an 'intellectual" and a target for certain death. When word leaked out that rebels would invade Embassies, all of the valuable documents were burned in the barrels that had been saved for this purpose.

Rebels confused hearing aids for radio transmitters communicating with American planes coming to bomb Congo. One Belgian was shot because he tapped his gold tooth and the rebels knew he was sending secret messages.

Soldiers at times were uncertain about their loyalties. They came to worship services at mission stations and asked if they could sleep there overnight. Yes. Curfew was 3:30 p.m. to 7 a.m. and all roads were closed.

Missionaries were told to get out while they could and Gordon and his partner Wes were available to transport them in their planes, but most of the missionaries felt safe because they were not political and were only in the country to serve the nationals. They were wrong about being safe.

A thousand people were killed in one city and the streets were piled with bodies massacred with machetes and spears, mutilated before the actual killing. Nurses were forced to bury the dead in piles of 50 to each common grave.

The treasury of Congo was empty. So was common sense and basic leadership. There was some humor, but not much. One doctor put out a sign that read: "Since your solders have stolen my car, all fees will now be double." His car was promptly returned.

The city of Stanleyville was in the south of the country 40 miles north of the equator. Gordon and Kathy and family were living in Leopoldville, 1,000 miles away. Stanleyville was an important city in part because the giant Congo River flowed through the city on its way to the sea and Stanley Falls was just beyond the city.

One hundred sixty missionaries in Stanleyville were unable to leave because rebels had taken all of the cars. They were going without food, too, because they had no money to buy it, but even if they had money, there was none to be bought in stores. Shop windows had been smashed and contents looted.

Some of the atrocities were too awful to describe. Simbas performed the kind of torture that can only be committed under the influence of drugs and serious hatred. At times a "Lieutenant" would demand keys to the missionary's car, but since the Lieutenant was 12 years old and had never driven a car, the missionary had to provide a quick lesson in driver's education.

Some missionaries hid in the jungle for weeks at a time afraid to stand in open spaces to signal to the MAF pilots that they were ready for rescue. Many were no longer afraid of death; they looked forward to being with the Lord.

Thousands of refugees fleeing from the jungle came across the Congo River into Stanleyville. People were sleeping everywhere; camps were filled, hotels overflowing. There was no rank. Everyone was poor.

The Congolese government had recruited mercenaries to fight for the cause, some of them with cancer hoping for a quick death, and others hoping for quick cash. The ones with a conscience or a weak stomach went home.

The American government considered sending in US heavily armed African-American soldiers to rescue US citizens, including the missionaries. In the end twelve planes, armored jeeps, 64 paratroopers, Air Force surgeons, and 320 soldiers arrived. They brought a hospital plane and 600 lbs. of medical equipment. The battle was bloody. 4,000 Congolese along with 28 priests and nuns were murdered by the Simbas.

The ones that made it to the airport were given a passport and a ticket home. Most of the refugees with white skin would be left in Congo, but it would be without a "decent burial."

President Johnson had just been elected President of the United States.

"We are not our own bosses to live or die as we ourselves might choose. Living or dying we follow the Lord. Either way we are his."
Romans 14:7-8 TLB

CHAPTER 31

How many Congolese died at the hands of the rebels was anyone's guess. Some said 40,000 and others believed 100,000 would be more accurate. Torrential rains failed to wash the steps of the Lumumba monument that was stained in blood. The rebels did not allow the burial of victims, so bodies were thrown into the river where crocodiles ate them.

In one village every man who wore trousers instead of a loincloth was killed. In another city the rebels burned so many bodies at the Lumumba monument that the sidewalk cracked under the heat of the 800 that were murdered that day. Some died from dismemberment, some were forced to drink gasoline and then their bodies were torched.

Sharon and Donny remember seeing bodies hanging on gallows in the city center, and dead bodies floating down the river behind the Baptist Mission Station house where they lived.

Leopoldville was destitute. Doctors had left and the hospitals were attended only by Congolese assistants. The entire country had practically no doctors. People were starving and starvation brought riots. Sanitary conditions were a low priority for Leopoldville's 350,000 people. There was no refrigeration because there was no electricity in hot Congo. Putrid meat and fish were dumped into the

Congo River. More crocodile food. Dogs had been tied up but they were starving, too weak to walk. The Congolese loved their dogs and could not shoot them. African street "courts" were shouting out whether the person was "good" or "bad." The bad ones were shot on the spot. It reduced the need for jail space.

Sharon, Donny and Darlene hid under their beds with the sounds of guns. When Kathy came to rebel guarded road blocks she simply told the children to put their "heads down" and she drove right through the barricades. They all understood the danger. They knew families who had lost everything to the rebels and Kathy had asked the children to give some of their meager supply of toys to children who had nothing.

Some of the missionary families came with young children and found playmates in Sharon, Donny and Darlene. These little "healers" also contributed to the emotional care of traumatized missionary kids who needed to play.

With so many stressed adults, the children could not help but hear some of the painful stories that were shared. Some stories were shared only in private, such as the rape of some of the women missionaries, but the children sensed the sadness. Although Sharon, Donny and Darlene had not encountered the rebels directly, they were exposed to the evil and fear that they brought and they were vicariously impacted.

The memories are still sharp in their minds 40 years later.

Some of the conversation of evacuating missionaries told of the faithfulness of Congolese Christians who chose to go to prison rather than abandon missionary women. All of the missionaries spoke of the sturdy faith of African believers that was displayed under pressure. These Africans met to pray and worship when it was dangerous to do so. They shared with others when they had little for themselves.

Initially, missionary run medical clinics had been treating rebel soldiers so missionaries felt safe because they were "neutral." That would change. Rebels increasingly demanded food, gas, money, radios and they were becoming increasingly hostile. Missionaries all over Congo knew they must evacuate or they would be killed.

The rebels would ask an African if he had butter. If the answer was yes, he was killed because it was clear he must have obtained the money for such an expensive item illegally. At Kindu 1500 civilians were killed and their bodies left on the beach for six days before being thrown into the Lualuab River.

Roman Catholic nuns and priests cared for Protestants missionaries and vice versa. At one time 67 Catholic and Protestant missionaries were crowded together to sleep on a bare floor. The rebels raped the nuns.

In the middle of this horror Gordon flew into the jungle in his red and white Cessna MAF plane searching for missionaries who wanted to be evacuated. He dropped messages with a trail of white bandage asking, "Are you in trouble? If everything is okay and you want to remain at your station, stand with your hands at your side. If there are signs of trouble and you plan to drive out, wave your hands above your head. If you want to be evacuated, sit on the ground. We will send a helicopter for you." The Cessna tilted, dipped one wing low, a gesture to signal that the pilot had received the missionary's message and then soared into the air.

During the crisis about 2,000 foreigners and hundreds of Congolese were airlifted to safety from NE Congo alone.

Gordon and Kathy had moved from the Baptist Mission Station to live at Union Mission House in downtown Leopoldville where Kathy would care for evacuating missionaries while they waited for flights out of the country. The hostel had a large table; wide breeze swept verandas, and had become a haven for evacuating missionaries.

In the dining room at mealtimes or on the upper veranda after breakfast or dinner they turned the old place into a sort of spiritual command post. No one understood more clearly the absolute necessity of prayer for fellow warriors still in the jungle. In addition, they swapped bits of news and told their own stories. Newsmen from all over the world dropped in at all hours to interview the refugees.

The men went to the American, Belgium and British embassies every day to remind the officials that folks in the interior still needed rescuing.

The Guest House had a capacity for 25 but during the rebel evacuations there were 50 sleeping there at times, including in the laundry room. Evacuees emerged from small air rescue planes or helicopters. They were bloody, unkempt, often distraught; some weeping hysterically and some speechless. They were on their way to Union Mission House and to Kathy's care.

Besides caring her three young children, there were now 50 hungry survivors, some needing unavailable medical care, all needing support, encouragement, and an ear to their story. Kathy had several hired Africans to assist with the daily chores and hardworking Joseph helped care for the children. Cooking was not one of his gifts.

Kathy waited in line each day for basic food supplies, helped with locating clothes, prepared meals for 50, changed sheets and did laundry for those leaving and waited for the new arrivals. Some evacuees would need help with obtaining passports and all would need tickets to their home countries. The missionaries spent about as much time at the Leopoldville airport as they did at UMH. Each plane might bring other missionaries for whom they were praying. They needed a warm hug and welcome when they arrived. They also needed the white sheets and bath that was waiting at UMH.

Gradually the number of residents at Union Mission House dwindled as families flew to their homes and to waiting relatives, home churches, and to safety. So much would change in that flight home, but one thing remained, they would continue to pray for Congolese they had come to love, and for families of those who would not need a flight home.

MAF suggested a move to a new station for Gordon and Kathy and family.

"For all the saints who from their labors rest,
Who thee by faith before the world confessed,
Thy name, O Jesus be forever blest,
Alleluia!"
-Leonard Harris

CHAPTER 32

Gordon and Kathy had lived in Leopoldville, a battle zone for three years when Missionary Aviation Fellowship offered to send them home for a break from the awful stress. Gordon wanted to finish their four-year term so the family was moved to Ubangi Province in NE Congo for a year prior to furlough in Fullerton. Ubangi was a tranquil retreat compared to the flying bullets and traumatized house guests of Leopoldvillle. Sharon was now 8, and a 3rd grader, Donny was 6 and in 1st grade, and Darlene was a busy 4-year old learning her colors and numbers. The children were settled in a local school and Kathy was concerned about causing more upheaval in their lives by a move to a new station, but she had nothing to fear, Karawa in Ubangi Province was as peaceful as it got in Congo during the Simba uprising. The peace didn't last long and rebels would desecrate the Province eventually, along with the rest of the country, but for now it was a sanctuary.

But it was not a luxury resort. Ubangi was one of the poorest and least developed Provinces in Congo. Some natives had never seen a plane. Karawa Station was built on a hill and the entrance sign read, "Mbote", the traditional Lingala greeting. The grounds were loaded with palm trees, tropical foliage and dirt roads that became mud holes during tropical down pours. Nights were cool. It might be a stretch to call it a tropical paradise unless you were comparing it to massacres in Leopoldville, and then it qualified.

There was a hospital, a church, and a nursing school for African nurses on the property. Acquiring clothes for growing children required trade with missionaries who had children 1 year older. There were no stores, unless you counted the "Post" which had some goods, but not what you needed. Kathy had tried to guess sizes for the children for 4 years. Sometimes that worked. Gordon could occasionally buy clothes where he flew his plane. Fortunately it was hot and not many clothes were needed.

Kathy would have help, a cook who didn't know how to cook and a housecleaner who didn't clean but did wash clothes. Gordon had a "helper" in the hanger, too. Help was hired not by resume and job qualifications, but based on the African person's need for a job.

Cooking was done on a wood stove and water was boiled and filtered. Ironing was with a charcoal iron. Bread was baked. Bargaining with the women who came to the house to sell their wares took time. Rice and spaghetti had to be tightly secured in tins, or the weevils ate them before the family. When an animal was butchered the family cut, ground, and packaged the meat. So much for the Safeway meat counter.

The family home at Karawa was a whitewashed mud structure with a sobi grass thatched roof which allowed insects and sometimes snakes or monkeys to fall through. A bucket on the porch provided showers. There was no indoor bathroom and it was a long walk to the outhouse so it was better to avoid the trip if possible at night since you might be joined by critters on the path. Later after Gordon and Kathy had lived there awhile an indoor bathroom was installed. The windows were screened and without glass. When a storm came, the shutters were closed. The house was one big open room with a separate bedroom for Gordon and Kathy. Sharon slept on an enclosed porch, and Donny and Darlene had a screened section. Kinsawa, the house help did the cooking.

The menu for dinner had an international flair and included black mamba snake, python, fried caterpillars, fried ants, and, termites. Gordon shot buffalo and Donny provided food by spear fishing and shooting birds and monkeys. Once he shot a bird with a 10 foot wing span and was chased by another bird of the same size that was encouraging him to back off. Don and Gordon went hippo hunting one time but did not manage to shoot one. Carrying it home would have been a challenge, anyway. There were piranhas in the river, which had an interest in toe nibbling. Donny learned to do taxidermy on some of the animals he shot.

The cook house was in the back of the property, along with the fruit and vegetables that Gordon planted which included sweet potatoes, manioc, bananas, mangos, and pineapple.

While Gordon and Don hunted and gathered, Sharon climbed trees in the back yard and read books. She also watched surgeries by means of the "Open Door" policy at the hospital. There was no privacy in the operating room. Anyone could walk in and watch for a while. Africans (and, Sharon) just had to see what was going on. One time she brought a newborn African baby home for care and for her mother to do the night feedings.

Also in the back yard were the critters who were adopted by the family including 2 baby crocodiles who lived happily in a tub until a large turtle crawled on the wood cover and drowned them. Many African gray parrots lived with them over the years, but their favorite, Jocko was the only one to come home with them to Salem at the end of their missionary service. Jocko spoke some Lingala by then, as well as knowing the first verse of most Christmas carols. Seriously, he did. He was one smart bird. There were a variety of monkeys who became pets but the favorite was Sammy. The geese served some purposes but cuddling was not one of them. Donald and Daisy Duck made messes, but were tame enough to avoid becoming roast ducks at Christmas.

Lingala was used for bartering and to instruct the house help so learning it was not optional. The Congolese did not understand any English or French although English was used at the mission school on the property. The family learned Lingala by pointing to objects and listening to the African say the word. The same word could have several dramatically different meanings depending on the tone used, such as "peanut" and "spear". Same word exactly, but get the tone wrong and the mistake was significant. Many words had potential to cause communication challenges or interesting sermons, depending on your perspective.

"We live within the shadow of the Almighty, sheltered by the God who is above all gods. This I declare, that he alone is my refuge, my place of safety. He is my God and I am trusting him."
Psalm 91:1 TLB

CHAPTER 33

Gordon flew his small plane to provide evacuation for missionaries who needed transport to safety and some who were ill and needed access to a hospital. At times he flew pregnant women in active but difficult labor who needed a doctor. These flights frequently included delivering precious mail, or, precious children ready to go home for vacation from the boarding school on the Karawa station. Between flights he serviced his plane. No one could have had a more skilled mechanic. Kathy managed the radio communication to the plane, notified the hospital of incoming patients, and encouraged Gordon who was sometimes gone from home two weeks at a time. Gordon maintained a detailed journal of his flights. He was a calm, experienced pilot.

When Gordon was at home he followed the news on the BBC station. Information about conditions in the rest of Congo was not good. No one expected the Simbas to come to this remote NE corner of Congo, but danger was getting closer as rebels followed the Congo River north.

In the evenings, families at Karawa gathered in the little chapel for brief services in English and a portable pump organ provided the music to familiar hymns. On Sunday mornings the service was led by a Congolese pastor and the sermon was in Lingala.

Sharon and Donny attended Ubangi Academy on the mission property, a school for the children of missionaries and Darlene, a very bright little girl was waiting for her turn to go to school although she already knew a lot that American children never learn. While she waited she would have to teach her monkey, Sammy, who had trouble staying at his desk.

At the beginning of the school year parents came with children who would be boarding at the dorms and they spent a few days getting acquainted with other missionary parents. It was a giant party (until the day the parents went home without their children and then the party went down the tube). The year that Sharon graduated from High School at Karawa, there were 10 seniors in the class and four of them became National Merit Scholars. The teaching was excellent and expectations high. Too much 1:1 attention in this small school to allow any laziness to go unnoticed!

Children came home from school for a big breakfast (papaya, oatmeal, powdered milk, eggs and toast), and then the main meal of the day was at lunch. Rice, greens, wild boar and a cookie was followed by a 2-hour nap, and then back to school. Supper came from canned goods that Kathy had previously prepared.

Kathy made birthday cakes in various shapes to honor those milestones. The house help bartered for some of the food. Salt was valuable and many of the

Congolese had goiters from lack of iodine in the salt.
A large fish weighing 36 lbs. sold for $3.

Evenings were short since it was dark by 6:30 p.m.,
but they were fun. Families on the station had more
time together than U.S, families since there were
fewer distractions. They played Scrabble, listened to
the tape recorder and made homemade root beer.
When Gordon was home he enchanted the kids with
his true adventure stories (based on his own growing
up in Gabon with missionary parents). The famous Dr.
Albert Schweitzer was his neighbor and the family
doctor. Gordon made and painted airplanes with
Donny. On Saturdays the family went to Kwada where
there was lake and the children could swim.

They rode in a pirogue, an entire tree trunk that has
been hollowed out and shaped to move swiftly in the
Ubangi River which had many whirlpools. These tree-
boats tipped over easily. The Ubangi River wound
through deep green dense jungle and crocodiles were
waiting. The Congolese said, "He is our enemy. He
ate our forefathers, he eats us, and now we eat him in
our anger." They also ate them because they tasted
good.

There were no appointments at the hospital on the
property. Many people walked for days to see a
doctor. The next closest hospital was 6 hours away by
truck and these trucks were infrequent and usually
already filled with others seeking care. Time meant

nothing to the Congolese. They would wait around the hospital for weeks to see the doctor. It was good to know in advance when you would become ill.

African nurses were unreliable and often drunk. Standards were low and an African nurse might walk into the operating room and take an instrument he needed to use on another patient. Night operations were performed by kerosene lanterns. The doctor saw 100 patients a day and care, or lack of care after surgery was provided by the family. Occasionally an autopsy was done but the stench of the decaying body could only be tolerated by inserting crushed pungent flowers into the doctor's nostrils.

Although Gordon and Kathy had no direct contact with Dr. Paul Carlson, he had studied Lingala at Karawa before going to his own station at Wasolo Hospital where he would be the only doctor for 100,000 people, so he was known at Karawa. Patients at the hospital paid what they could, anywhere from 1 cent a day for antibiotics to nothing at all. The generosity of American drug companies who donated medicines to mission hospitals made healing drugs available.

Dr. Carlson was captured by the Simbas and imprisoned at a convent with 31 priests and 15 nuns for a time and then eventually he was shot and his body was left alongside the road. His body was eventually flown back to Karawa, to a place where he was loved for burial. He was deeply respected for his servant life. "He stripped himself of all privilege in order to become a servant." Philippians 2:5

Gordon and Kathy spent two 4-year terms, plus the final year of their first term at Karawa. Each furlough was spent in Fullerton at the MAF headquarters. When Sharon graduated from High School and was ready for college the family chose to retire to Salem, where Gordon's parents lived, rather than be separated from 17-year old Sharon.

Rebels advanced and in time invaded this beautiful northeast corner of Congo, but there had always been some darkness in this "heart of Africa" even before the rebels came, which brought sadness and concern for missionary families.

Female circumcision was practiced here. Young girls were taken by women into the forest and made to dance until they were in a frenzy and then the circumcision was performed. Girls were told that without this procedure no one would marry them and they would be considered a whore by the village. If the girl cried during the excruciating procedure the assisting women shamed her. Christianity brought an end to this torture and disrespect of women and the practice was eventually outlawed.

Witch doctors had great power over villagers. When Sharon was 16-years old she went alone to visit a witch doctor in order to ask questions that were of concern to her. He demonstrated his dance and put himself into a trance and then suddenly stopped and told her she needed to leave. She was happy to comply and aware that God had protected her.

Living in Congo presented a variety of risks. During their years in Leopoldville Sharon and Donny and Darlene were all bitten by a rabid dog and were subjected to a series of 14 painful rabies shots in their abdomens.

Polygamy was common with villagers and husbands often had a favorite wife and children. Again, Christianity brought change to this long-standing marriage practice.

And, since Congo was primarily a Catholic country at the time, there was some resentment and hostility at the invasion of these Protestants who might steal the Catholic flock. Jesuits stood in trucks pointing guns at children who were leaving a Catholic school to attend the Protestant one. This tension did not affect Gordon's practice of rescuing Catholics in danger, however, and during the Simba uprising he rescued 100 Protestant and Catholic missionaries alike.

Dominican Sisters and priests from France had a station near Karawa and Sharon went to visit them with the reluctant approval of Gordon, and the confident approval of Kathy. They invited her to spend Spring break with them and Sharon went with a friend. She describes the visit as "so much fun." In the evenings the nuns and priests who were teachers at the Catholic school, drank beer and played cards. They had a secret swimming hole where the nuns wore fewer clothes than their traditional habits. Sharon went to mass with them. They were kind to her and Sharon left with a sense of friendship for her neighbors and realized that these were good people who also loved Christ.

The move to Oregon came when Sharon was 17, Don, 15, and Darlene, 13 years old. The adjustment would not be easy for these teenagers who had never had spending money, shopped for clothes at The Gap, heard pop artists, gone to movies, or used the current slang. Oregon was different from the jungle. Not better. Just different.

> "We should make our plans –
> counting on God to direct us."
> Psalm 16:9 TLB

CHAPTER 34

As a young boy Gordon had traveled on foot for three months at a time through 700 miles of dense jungle with his Dad to present the Gospel in Gabon. Even then Gordon knew that it would be so much easier to travel by plane.

Independence had not only destroyed the roads in Congo, it had taken the sense of safety from missionaries, especially those with young children, so the presence of MAF pilots provided the security that was needed when emergency evacuation was necessary. Gordon became a bridge to life.

During the Simba uprising Gordon and the other MAF pilot, Wes Eisenmann, flew courageously into treacherous danger to rescue missionaries from peril. There were four flying outfits in Congo at the time providing rescue services: the UN, Air Brussels, Air Congo, and MAF. All of the other planes were hit by bullets and although the MAF planes were frequently shot at, no bullet ever hit the MAF planes.

The stories of persecution by the heroic missionaries who survived will never be fully told since missionaries tend to make light of their suffering. In addition Congolese Christians by the hundreds suffered and risked their lives for the sake of the missionaries they loved.

It would be fair to ask why the country of Congo has had almost continuous vicious outbursts of lawlessness, fighting, and blood shed, civil wars, brutal murders, assassinations, rebellions, ethnic strife and political instability? Today it is dangerous to travel in the Democratic Republic of Congo, formerly Zaire, and before that, Congo. Even the name changes tell the story of constant upheaval.

The Simbas are gone, but the political and social, and moral challenges remain when the truth of the Gospel has been proclaimed throughout Congo for the past 150 years. Has it made a difference? The answer(s) are no doubt more complex than two simple responses to that observation, but it is clear as Jesus followers that a) we are to be obedient to the Great Commission to share the Gospel, and b) the result of obedience does not come with a written guarantee. Obey and let go of the results.

Kathy was the resident "Chief Mental Health Officer" for scores of severely traumatized adult missionaries and their children for a period of many months. The cost of that ministry was not only incurred by her but also by the three young children in the family, who carried into adulthood fresh memories of the violence they saw, heard, and felt.

Years later, Sharon, Gordon and Kathy's oldest daughter married Ralph and they were accepted by the Mennonite Central Committee to serve three years in Kenya where Ralph would teach Bible in a Muslim school. He had earned a MA in Old Testament from Western Seminary, in Portland, Oregon.

After only three weeks in Kenya on Sept 9, 1982 Sharon and Ralph and 6-month-old baby Anya were returning from Mombassa when they ran into a stalled truck left abandoned on the road. It was a road without lights, of course. Two teachers in the back seat and Ralph were killed. Sharon was severely injured with a dislocated hip, badly mangled arm, and severe nose and facial lacerations. It took 15 hours to get her to a hospital. Anya was unharmed, but lay with an unconscious mother and three dead adults in the pitch dark for hours until help came.

The Mennonite Central Committee provided an airplane ticket for Kathy to go to Nairobi and care for Sharon and Anya at the African hospital for months until Sharon could be safely transported to the U.S. Ralph was buried near Rift Valley Academy outside of Nairobi where he had attended school. He was 28 years old. Kathy attended his service.

> "The Lord is close to those whose hearts are breaking."
> Psalm 34:18 TLB

CHAPTER 35
Kathy's Story

Kathy was born Feb 10, 1934 with Mrs. Wu, midwife assisting. It was the Chinese New Year so she was welcomed with fireworks and celebrations. The weather in Tianshui was bitter cold and the family's calf froze to death the month before her birth so Malcolm skinned the calf and stuffed it with straw. The cow began licking the calf and giving plenty of milk. The rabbits also froze to death and the family ate them. Hopefully the bunnies didn't have names.

As a child Kathy lived 4 ½ years separated from her parents while she attended Chefoo School. She entered school at 5 ½ years and did not see her parents again until she was 10 years old and was reunited with them and her younger twin siblings in Albany, Oregon.

She finished school in Albany and graduated from Albany High School. Following high school she attended Seattle Pacific College where she worked in the dining hall cleaning tables. A handsome young man was a late eater and they found time to talk. Kathy said she approached him with the comment that their parents knew each other and were both missionaries. That line works every time! Soon they were dating and Gordon was warned by his roommate that HE wanted to date Kathy so he better not mess up. Gordon gave Kathy a watch as a gift early in their courtship and his parents noted that it was "too early" for such a serious gift, but apparently not for Gordon! He proposed, but Kathy turned him down initially, but came to her senses and said yes the next time he asked. They were engaged the summer of Kathy's first year, and married after her sophomore year. Gordon was a 20 year old junior at the time. He graduated from SPU and Kathy quit school to work and assist with expenses as well as to be Mommy to baby Sharon who was born the summer after Gordon graduated.

Gordon and Kathy anticipated missionary service with the Christian and Missionary Alliance and began the required two years of church ministry in preparation for overseas work at a church at Bainbridge Island, Washington. After they were there seven months, Gordon heard about the work of Missionary Aviation Fellowship. It was hard to imagine being "called" by God to do something he would LOVE to do. Go figure!

He took the necessary mechanic and flight training and they lived in Fullerton, California at the MAF headquarters until Gordon was fully prepared to be a jungle pilot and then the family, which now included Donny and Darlene along with big sister, Sharon left with their parents for Switzerland and language school prior to going to Congo.

After completing their service in Congo the family settled in Salem to be near Gordon's parents and

Kathy worked as a receptionist at Salem Alliance Church. Sharon and Don Jr. live in Salem, too and both have wonderful Christian families who have heard the stories of growing up in Africa. Darlene died from Leukemia at age 27 years.

Jocko, their African gray parrot sang Christmas carols at the family gatherings, and spoke some Lingala when he was not in the mood to sing.

"When peace like a river attendeth my way,
When sorrows like sea billows roll,
Whatever my lot, Thou hast taught me to say,
It is well; it is well with my soul."
-Horatio Spafford

CHAPTER 36

Blonde, smart, and kind Lillian Amstutz arrived in Vietnam to serve as a missionary nurse with the Christian and Missionary Alliance in January of 1958. She studied the language in Dalat where she was also in charge of the medical clinic which served the local tribes people. She delivered 25 babies between studies. No doubt she learned the word for "ouch" early on. Her ability to stay awake all night to welcome babies and focus on learning the language in the day time is a testament to her intelligence as well as her ability to function well while sleep deprived!

After she completed language study she went to the Banmethuot Leprosarium to work and to study the Rade language. The Leprosarium treated lepers who lived in the jungles, often alone and separated from their families. The CMA constructed a large building on 150 acres of land for these lepers.

Richard arrived in Vietnam in December of 1958, 12 months after Lillian's arrival. They had begun a courtship mostly by mail. He obviously had a way with words and two years later they were married at Dalat, the site of the school for missionary children. It was October, 1960.

Richard had studied Vietnamese for a year in Pleiku. After Richard and Lillian were married they went to a small town in the hills above Quang Ngai and together they began learning the Hre language, but Communist forces threatened the areas and they were moved to Banmethuot, 70 miles north of Dalat.

The Bunong tribe, south of Banmethuot was experiencing a hunger for God and Richard and Lillian were sent to provide the Scriptures and Christian teaching.

The country of Vietnam has been described as shaped like a long dragon. The head spreads around Hanoi. The body covers the coastal flats, tribal highlands and Mekong Delta. The tail curls into the Gulf of Siam about 225 miles north of Malaysia.

In the late 1940's the Nationalist Party (the Viet Minh) founded by Ho Chi Minh was formed in an effort to defeat French rule in Viet Nam. They called themselves, The League for the Independence of Viet Nam, and by 1953 the rule of France was crumbling and the Viet Minh were gaining power. The French battled the stubborn Viet Minh guerillas, but it was becoming a losing battle. The Viet Cong was the military arm of this Communist movement. Richard and Lillian arrived in Vietnam five years later and there would be no welcome signs posted by the VC to acknowledge their arrival.

Christian and Missionary Alliance missionaries had been in Vietnam since 1911 and by 1940 there were

161 congregations. The story of the evangelical church in Vietnam reads like the book of Acts. The church doubled in size each year. Some of the early missionaries befriended Ho Chi Minh in his younger years. He heard the Gospel and rejected it.

Prior to the growing military conflict missionaries worked throughout all of Vietnam, mainly in rural areas. That would change as the war advanced. The United States did not support dividing the country into north and south and a declaration of war was issued. In 1961 the first US troops arrived, sent by President Kennedy.

But the Viet Cong was becoming more aggressive and violent and 1 million refugees fled from the north into South Viet Nam. They came needing housing, food, and, medicine. Catholic Relief Services and the Mennonites helped The Christian and Missionary Alliance staff. Missionaries could no longer work in the north.

The Vietnam War was the longest in US history. It lasted 6 years and 6 months, 24 hours longer than the Revolutionary War. Americans know more and understand less about the Vietnam War than any other war in our history. 25,000 young adults died in the jungles and rice paddies 10,000 miles from home and often came home to a lack of respect and honor.

Missionaries who came to serve the people also died. More than any other group missionaries were hated, hounded, and tortured. Vietnamese pastors were buried alive, as well as innocent teens that were accused of being, "American Imperialist Agents." It would not be long before Richard and Lillian would become "guests" of the Viet Cong, a hospitality better refused if that was an option, and it wasn't.

"Some nations boast of armies and of weaponry, but out boast is in the Lord our God."
Psalm 20:7 TLB

CHAPTER 37

Vietnamese mountain people were short, brown and small. The men wore loincloths and the women wore long black skirts and colorful tops. The children wore nothing, which kept their laundry to a minimum. The people's belief in the power of evil spirits was intense and dictated most decisions of life. One man named his four sons, Lizard, Snake, Drunkard, and Dung. Now THAT would scare the evil spirits away! The people cowered in fear at the sight of a rainbow because they believed that an evil spirit lived at the end of it. So much for the pot of gold!

Goats, pigs and chickens ran freely until they were sacrificed for bloody feasts. The animals were killed slowly by spears because suffering pleased the evil spirits. Bowls caught the blood that was then sprinkled on sick relatives and rubbed on the doorposts of houses. If a mother died in childbirth the still alive baby was buried with her in a hollow log to appease the evil spirits.

The year was 1962 and the Viet Cong were becoming increasingly brazen. No one knew when soldiers might emerge from the jungle, spear in hand and go on a killing rampage. The tension was high and the proximity of these wild men close. They were camped just outside of Banmethuot, but so was a US military station. Wycliffe translators were killed and Catholic nuns shot. There were 2,000 assassinations and 7,000 kidnappings that year.

The Viet Cong kidnapped three Christian missionaries known and loved by Richard and Lillian: Archie Mitchell, Dan Gerber, and Dr. Ardel. They were never heard from again. No one wondered if it was safe to be in Vietnam because it wasn't. One missionary said that he was not there for the adrenaline rush. He had a job to do and he could do it best if he remained alive. No missionaries resigned. No one asked to be transferred to another country. They all believed that there were worse things than going to heaven a few years early.

The war increased in 1964 with the bombing of an US aircraft carrier in Saigon harbor. Guerillas ambushed a truck carrying 40 women and children near the CMA station and 6 women and 5 children were stabbed to death, 21 others wounded. The guerillas carved out their hearts. Battles near Banmethuot took 240 lives. Death was in the air and Richard and Lil knew they could be killed at any time. They traveled in busses marked with a cross and "CMA" painted on the side.

The more the persecution, the more the churches grew. South of Banmethuot the tribal congregation climbed to over 1,000 members.

Life was so uncertain for nationals that parents delayed naming their babies after they were born until they were several months old. No need to waste a name on a child that would not survive.

There were cratered fields all over the country. In one year the US dropped 637,000 tons of bombs on Vietnam, 5 tons for every square mile. The escalation of the war brought an increase in suffering refugees pouring into the south.

In the tension and chaos of "bombs bursting in air," Richard and Lil quietly worked on the Mnong language and avoided all things political. They were surrounded by roving, hostile armies who were intensely political, however, and who were motivated to capture Banmethuot, the capitol of the Province.

Newspapers all over the world carried the story of the three captured missionaries and the staff at CMA headquarters did what they could to gain their release, but so far nothing had worked. The call of God to obedience whether by life or death was quietly re-affirmed by all of the missionaries.

> "Thy way, O Lord, not mine,
> However dark it be,
> Lead me by Thine own hand,
> Choose out the path for me."
> -Horatius Bonar

In early January, Richard and Lil left Banmethuot to attend a literacy conference at the Wycliffe

Translation Center and the other missionaries remained at the station. It was the Tet New Year celebration, Christmas and July 4th rolled into one for the Vietnamese, but a little bit quieter at the literacy conference.

The Communists knew better than to violate this special holiday and the people could finally "come up for air" from the war and they could light the long strings of fire crackers which would protect themselves from the evil spirits since the good spirits took a trip to the stars just before Tet.

The reality was that the VC had moved into strike position for the deadliest battle of the war so far, Tet or no Tet. A General of the North Vietnamese army was quoted as saying, "The life and death of human beings means nothing."

Soldiers charged suddenly into the streets with gunfire and rockets. US Marines arrived within minutes and a 3-½ hour bloody battle followed. Execution teams went door to door and shot families.

Gunfire reached the Translation Center where Richard and Lil were working and children were hurried into bunkers. One bullet flew 18 inches from Richard's head.

At 3 a.m. bombs and grenades awakened the missionaries and the local US military advisors told them to get out immediately. A pilot directed the missionaries to a helicopter. They grabbed their translation materials and ran. As they ran they could hear the screams of the wounded and dying. The center was bombed as they lifted into the air. That night 960 VC were shot dead by US forces.

There was no news about the Banmethuot missionaries back at their station. Those missionaries were hiding in shelters, some with three inches of water and full of rats. Their water supply was down to 1 cup per person per day. Food was limited to a tiny amount of C rations. Some missionaries were located by American military staff and evacuated. Civilians were shot in the back of the head or buried alive. The group of missionaries in shelters painted SOS on top of Richard and Lillian's car along with a white flag but it was never seen, at least not by the "good guys."

By Friday, the news of the massacre of the six martyred missionaries was known and the news reached the boarding school where the children of the missionaries were staying. The children had no news about their parents, but the awareness that they either were already orphans or could be soon was obvious.

Twelve days later Richard was back at Banmethuot. He heard the deep sorrow of the pilots at the military base because they had been unable to save the missionaries' lives. The houses of all of the missionaries had been looted. Richard gathered a few personal items and near a bunker a page from a hymnbook with the song:

"Anywhere with Jesus I can safely go
Anywhere he leads me in this world below, Anywhere
without Him dearest joys would fade
Anywhere with Jesus, I am not afraid."
-Jessie Pounds

The next day he returned to find the bodies of his co-workers face down, killed by gunshot or grenades. Richard and co-workers buried the bodies, and a brief service was held with Scripture read and Richard closed in prayer. GI's planted a rough wooded cross at the site.

At a service held in the US, the President of The Christian and Missionary Alliance said, "The romance and the glory of the missionary call had long since departed. They had lived in the midst of war for many years. They had watched three of their comrades being led away into the jungle, never to be seen again. They knew they were vulnerable. They chose to be faithful, even unto death."

"Soldiers of Christ arise, and put your armor on,
Strong in the strength, which God supplies, through
His eternal Son. Strong in the Lord of Hosts, And in
His mighty power, who in the strength of Jesus trusts,
Is more than conqueror."
-Charles Wesley

CHAPTER 38

Richard and Lillian continued their translation work in Banmethuot. The war raged on with rockets passing overhead, some close enough to throw dirt on the roof of the pink house where they lived.

They had been told to contact Paul Struharick, the US Consul who lived near-by in the event of an emergency, and the current situation qualified. Without being dramatic, this was life or death.

Richard was exhausted and they were all deeply grieving the recent death of their friends and co-workers. The main road out of the city had been cut and Communist forces had barricaded the mountain passes. There was no access to gasoline or food, and there was also no way out of town.

Richard had a visit from a government official who warned that it was likely the Communists would take over the city soon and he advised the missionaries to get out NOW! He didn't say how they were going to do that.

Everyone was packed and ready to go if a way opened. Maybe a flight on a government plane? In the meantime Paul advised them to move to his house.

They hid in a downstairs bedroom with Richard on the bed, looking pale and exhausted. With them in the bedroom was Peter, who worked with the Australian

Broadcasting Company and was interested in tribal language broadcasting, and Jay, a Cornell student, who had made the unfortunate decision to visit a friend in Banmethuout for one day. Big mistake.

One small candle lit the room, no window, no electricity. They flushed the toilet during air strikes. There was no radio contact to American military personnel. There were 16 in the room; one was 5-year-old LuAnne, daughter of missionaries who worked closely with Richard and Lillian.

They discussed their options, none of them good ones. They could wait until the Viet Cong found them, or they could walk out carrying a white flag made from a pillowcase and hope that a helicopter saw them before the Viet Cong, definitely a long shot.

They made the white flag and carried a "Don't Shoot" sign. Once exposed the Viet Cong were in charge. The new POWs were told that they could carry small bags and a gallon of water. Their destination was unknown, but it would not be an itinerary chosen by the missionaries. They were now in the custody of the "Liberation Armed Forced of Vietnam". The soldiers took the jewelry of their new guests and provided a receipt. It was March of 1975. Jay commented that the last thing the Nazis did before sending the Jews to the gas chamber was to give them a receipt for their possessions.

The trail out of town was rough and it was the middle of the night before they were allowed to stop at a clearing. This would be "Motel Six" minus some of the amenities such as beds. They would not be alone. A huge number of prisoners were brought in during the night. Richard was near collapse.

In the morning Lil studied the printing on the dry combat rations and tried to figure how much would be needed to meet minimum daily nutritional requirements. It was not adequate and there would be even less food in the days ahead.

A guard gave them a list of questions and warned them not to lie because, "The Revolution knows everything." Questions included listing all of the places they had ever lived since birth, and describing their thoughts when they were being captured.

The restroom facilities were a bit primitive. Lil held up her skirt while the women used the latrine, a hole in the ground, but soon the whole field became a toilet and they named their new quarters, "The Rose Garden." Severely wounded and untreated prisoners groaned and cried around them. They stepped over bodies coming and going each time they moved.

They made their own chopsticks from bamboo, which was growing at the edge of the clearing. Their gallon of water was now gone and the stream was polluted, but they were given permission to boil water as long as there was no fire at night. Food would be rice cooked in large vats over an open fire. There would be no meat, fruit, or vegetables, just rice.

The Rose Garden was a temporary stay and they were told they would be moving. They were tied with ropes and transported by trucks to "Camp Sunshine" where there was a pile of thatch that was designated as their new sleeping quarters, no foam mattresses in sight.

They were also told that they could follow any religion they wanted as long as their primary loyalty was to the State. Given this "religious freedom" they were also advised that they could read their Bibles and hold quiet worship services on Sunday.

Multiple 9' by 12' shacks without walls, surrounded by bamboo poles were their living quarters. Each "enclosure" housed 50-60 prisoners. Openings were guarded and a path led to the river. A large hole had been dug for building fires to cook rice and a small amount of "soup" consisting of water and grease. Occasionally leaves were added to the soup, maybe for that final decorative touch.

A gong sounded at 5 a.m. and another gong when it was time for the prisoners to begin work. Prisoners were given permission to walk to the river to bathe. Lil shared her one tube of shampoo with everyone.

Day after day truckloads of new prisoners arrived. Within two weeks the population in camp was 1,000. Organization broke down, the latrine became inadequate, and confusion grew.

The guards did not offer their names so the missionaries assigned titles. The camp commander was, "Our Glorious Leader", the guard responsible for issuing permission to take a bath, "Bath Man."

The precious manuscripts that represented years of tedious work by these Bible translators were mostly gone...some left behind, some "in the (not) safe keeping of the Viet Cong, and a few were brought along in their bags. Richard and Lil committed their work to God and let go. They had been obedient to do what God had called them to do. It was God's Word, not theirs.

The group passed the time reading and memorizing Scripture, playing Pit and Sorry. Lil looked for butterflies, which she wanted to save for their children, and she played with little LuAnne.

The rainy season was just about to arrive so with any sign of rain, the remaining precious manuscripts were hidden under tarps. Rain meant sleeping on wet ground in the company of snakes and the likely possibility of being bitten by scorpions, bites that were excruciatingly painful.

They were given several cans of powdered milk and the cans themselves became treasured utensils. Once they cooked two tiny fish which the men caught one day while bathing, and they used the cans for making "rice coffee", which required some imagination, although it was brown. Weeds were cooked, too and with enough distraction and enough hunger, they could pretend it was spinach.

All of the parents had prepared wills and designated caregivers for their children. They assumed that their children had been sent from their boarding school to these relatives in their home countries. A guard announced that a plane had crashed and killed all of the children on board. It was a painful possibility that some of their own children had been on that flight. None of the missionaries were afraid to die, but leaving their children, now that was a terrible prospect.

Twice a day the prisoners were counted, although escaping from this jungle camp did not hold much promise.

Every day they were taken to a hut for hours of interrogation. The same questions over and over. The guards wanted detailed answers.

By now the group was starving, sick with high fevers, sore throats, and Lil was seriously ill. They were uncertain about what lay ahead. Many were beginning to assume they would die in the jungle and some said it out loud, "I don't think I will make it out alive."

Then they were told that they would be moved again. This time to "Camp Wilderness." They headed out to the main Ho Chi Minh trail. They were going north.

"On the day when I was weakest, they attacked.
But the Lord held me steady."
Psalms 18:18 TLB

CHAPTER 39

They were told they were being taken to "better facilities." A better camp could mean anything, but an improvement over the last camp was the least likely possibility.

Forty prisoners crowded into a Russian made truck with an open back. The heat was almost unbearable. Their heads were gashed by branches and their clothes torn as they threaded through the dense jungle.

When they stopped for lunch there was no restaurant in sight so they were given cold balls of rice. They stood in the stream and splashed water on their bodies but the "lunch break" ended and they were told that the rest of the "short distance" would be on foot. "Short" was a euphemism for an unknown distance, but it was always a lengthy and difficult hike. They would carry mosquito nets, tarps, manuscripts and bodies that were almost too weak to stand upright.

As they walked they were attacked by swarms of "fire ants" which completely ate through the rubber soles of their flip-flops.

They arrived at their new camp and it didn't look good. Definitely worse than before. The guards were hostile, food rations cut, and work was required of all prisoners for all day. Loud speakers blared the triumphal capture of Saigon and the news that it had been "liberated."

Some of the work was to build a fence around the camp "to keep unauthorized people from trying to come in." It was unclear how much problem the VC had incurred with folks breaking in.

The missionary group was starving and sick. Little LuAnne had a high temperature, Jay had an abscessed knee, Paul had a fungus infection, and another missionary had malaria. When one of the prisoners in camp died, some medicine was reluctantly provided for LuAnne. The hair of the missionaries was now falling out in large globs due to diet deficiencies. All of them were depressed.

The river provided a more private spot for bathing where they could actually take their clothes off. It had been awhile. Richard and Lillian provided toilet paper from copies of their manuscripts.

By now Lil had developed malaria. The other missionary's temperature had reached 105. Little LuAnne was desperately ill too, and finally was given permission for her mother to go with her by truck to the VC jungle "hospital," a facility yet to receive a 5-star rating. The truck slid off of the road during the trip but they all arrived, soaking wet from sweat, thirst and exhaustion. The latrine was 200 yards away, a significant hike, but perhaps it was a part of the

"Physical Therapy" rehab program?

After their return to camp two weeks later they were again told they would be moving to a new site. This one would be known as "Fat City."

Again, a stockade surrounded the new camp. Prisoners from another jungle camp would join them and during the night gaunt, emaciated, sick POWs arrived. Some of them had collapsed on the trail and had to be carried into camp.

Morale was at an all-time low. Most of the POWs had malaria and were desperately ill. The guards said that one person from the missionary group could walk to a village market and buy food. It was 4 miles each way and only Paul had enough strength to make the trip and carry back supplies. A guard would go too, of course.

Paul bought some fresh fruit and vegetables, and some prized toilet paper. In the weeks ahead they would be given a little powdered milk and some dog food to eat.

The rainy season had arrived and the men built troughs to carry water away from the sleeping quarters. The central open space became a giant mud hole. The rain brought snakes and rats into the housing area in search of food crumbs.

At night the gates were locked and the guards were outside the enclosure so the group sat around the fire talking and singing, "Home on the Range," and "Waltzing Matilda." On the 4th of July they sang, "God Bless America" and "America, The Beautiful." One of the missionaries began copying the books of the New Testament by hand.

Malaria had re-occurred for Lil. In addition she had developed a severe carbuncle on her back and eye. She was seriously ill and she was not sure she would live long. Camp officials decided to move her to the "hospital" where little LuAnne had been treated. Richard was allowed to go with her so she would not have to die alone. The "ambulance" consisted of 6 POW's and a canvas tied to a long pole.

The mass of carbuncles on Lil's back was removed at the hospital leaving a hole the size of a fist. The infection had already spread to other locations on her body. She would be in the hospital for 44 days. She left weak, but improved. Jay continued to weaken and he was also carried to the hospital.

While the three were at the hospital the camp was again moved. This time to "Potato Patch Camp." The announcement came without warning, as usual.

The roof over the sleeping area at the new camp was not rainproof and beds were soaked along with all of their belongings. Guards gave conflicting orders. Yes, you may get water. No, you may not. Discipline for non-compliance to orders included being placed in stocks, kneeling or standing in the hot sun, or being "deprived of privileges." The list of "privileges" was yet to be posted.

Richard and Lil observed some similarities between the Viet Cong and Christian commitment. They too gathered every night to sing their revolutionary songs and read Communist literature. They were willing to sacrifice for the cause of world revolution. One difference was that their cause was obtained by force and only Christian faith could change the heart.

Both Richard and Lil sought opportunities to talk to the guards and officers about their faith in Christ and they gave a doctor in camp their Modern English Translation Bible.

So far they had been prisoners of the Viet Cong for six months. They longed to hear that their children were safe, to know that that would be released not killed, and, to let their families in the States know that they were alive. A bath would be nice.

"So if you are suffering according to God's will, keep doing what is right and trust yourself to the God who made you, for he will never fail you."
I Peter 4:19 TLB

CHAPTER 40

On August 13, they were told that they would be moving again. That night Richard and Lillian, weak, pale and exhausted walked into camp from their hospital stay. Richard guessed that they would be moving to Hanoi, but helpful, truthful information was hard to come by. It was only the Americans that would be leaving, they did know that.

The missionaries traveled by truck for a week and finally stopped at an army barracks, which would be their new temporary home away from home. Four days later the rest of their small group arrived.

Meals were an improvement. Cabbage soup, tomatoes and one egg each was significantly better than eating almost nothing. They were locked in at night and not allowed to leave their room, but there was the tiny beginning of hope that the end of this nightmare was coming.

After a week, travel continued into North Vietnam and pictures of Ho Chi Minh's face were plastered on every blank wall. At night they slept in various army camps and 14-hour days were spent in the back of a truck. Baths were in irrigation ditches.

Five days later they arrived at the next camp and were given the rules, which included getting up at 5:00 a.m., the same schedule as at other camps.

They asked how many prisoners were in the camp and were told that there were none; they only had "guests." The "guests" were emaciated, desperately ill, untreated, and wondering how much longer they could survive. One of the missionaries had severe dysentery, another serious infection; another one had stomach pain, and yet another, malaria. One of the women was taken to the hospital with severe vomiting and pain. Little LuAnne was very ill with a high fever, vomiting, sore throat, and diarrhea. One missionary woman had lost 55 lbs. They were a sorry sight. Officials at the new camp decided that food rations must be increased because this group might make the Viet Cong look bad. Really?

Daily interrogations increased in frequency and intensity. Their rooms were searched. Richard returned one day to announce to the group that finally he had been told his crime. They had told him he was "too good, and it might make people think that Americans were good people." Richard reminded them that they had been exposed to enough Americans to know that some were NOT good.

Interrogations including being asked to list the names of all members of their mission organization and where each one lived, what language they studied, and what printed material had been produced. They were to write their life story, and, describe how they felt about their prison experience. The sessions were hostile, accusatory, and the demand to reveal their real espionage activity in Vietnam as well as their roles in the CIA, were expected. Richard was told that he wouldn't be released until he condemned U.S. foreign policy in Vietnam. Apparently providing name, rank and serial number was insufficient data to satisfy the Viet Cong.

The interrogations took place in a shed on the property. Norman Johnson, one of the captured missionaries tells in the book, *Prisoners of Hope*, about a cow that was brought in by truck, no doubt to provide milk for the guards. "Bossy" was allowed to wander freely throughout the camp and she regularly wandered into the interrogation room to "do her duty". The communist interrogators found the stench to be too much, so the grillings had to be delayed or temporarily eliminated while the space was cleaned and aired. The missionaries came to refer to the source of their reprieve as, "Holy Cow." She provided the relief the missionaries desperately needed. Perhaps in their evening worship the little group sang, "All Creatures of Our God and King," I don't know. I do know that all creatures are His, including "Bossy."

Besides the daily interrogations they were taken on several "cultural interest" trips in Hanoi, such as to, The National Museum of Natural History. They would have preferred a "cultural trip" to a restaurant. In the evenings they watched East German movies about racial oppression in the U.S. The officials took all of their papers including Richard's doctoral dissertation, which was ready for submission to Cornell University. Jewelry was taken, for "safe keeping."

They were measured for new clothes because the clothes they were wearing were made in South Vietnam and that would not be "appropriate." Their footprints were collected for new shoes. They were treated for worms. A doctor examined Lil who was having trouble breathing. He didn't know the cause.

Finally they were told to type their request for release and they were given NORTH Vietnamese shirts and trousers, appropriate clothing. Paul, the U.S. Consul official, endured terrible interrogations and was separated from the missionaries. When he was allowed to rejoin them he said that they had tried to make him acknowledge that the missionaries were a cover organization for an intelligence operation. Paul gave them a little talk about differences in life style between him and the missionaries (wine, women and song, probably) to help the Viet Cong understand. Paul was also accused of trying to organize the missionaries but he assured them that "NO ONE could organize THAT bunch!"

The last Sunday the group met to thank God for their survival. They sang, "Loved with Everlasting Love", and Richard sang a solo of, "The Love of God."

Their jewelry was returned but none of the manuscripts of translated Scripture or Richard's dissertation. Several of the missionaries begged for their return while others in the group cried. Richard stood silently and acknowledged that his dissertation belonged to God not to him.

As they climbed on the bus at 6:15 a.m. to be taken to the airport they were given bamboo purses, combs, perfume and Vietnamese hats, soap, toothpaste and hand towels, items which would have been helpful a few months earlier.

They had spent eight months in captivity. On board the plane they were given a sandwich, a tangerine, a coke and a cupcake. When the plane stopped for re-fueling they were able to make phone calls and actually talk to their children who were safe with relatives in the United States.

They were met in Bangkok by the U.S. Ambassador to Thailand and a press conference followed. They were just becoming aware of the worldwide interest in what had happened to them. They looked at press releases about the untiring efforts to bring them home.

They briefly walked the streets in Bangkok and ate at a restaurant although they were overwhelmed by the choices and couldn't tolerate much food. The evening ended with a bath, a real bath that included soap. Eight months of dirt would take a while to soak off.

They were issued new passports, and finally the time came to say goodbye to those who had endured the hardship with them. They would board separate planes and head home, shaky, weak, sick…but heading home and to their children.

"We live within the shadow of the Almighty, sheltered by the God who is above all gods. This I declare, that he alone is my refuge, my place of safety; he is my God, and I am trusting him."
Psalms 91:1-2 TLB

CHAPTER 41

Fast-forward 40 years:

Refugees from the Bunong tribe that Richard and Lillian had served in Vietnam had been coming to the U.S. for sanctuary and many had settled in North Carolina.

Richard's translation of the Scripture and hymnbook had been almost completed prior to being captured by the Viet Cong. They had carried, guarded, protected the precious manuscripts during their POW incarceration but in the end they were all confiscated by the Communists and never returned. They were left with releasing them to God.

Richard earned a Doctorate degree while they were in the United States. Later, they were reassigned by The Christian and Missionary Alliance, to serve in Burkina Faso, West Africa until retirement 19 years later.

Richard and Lillian retired in the U.S. in 1998. Once they were settled, the invitation came from the North Carolina refugees to come and visit them. Richard and Lillian were eager to be with these loved people who they had not seen in so many years. There was incredible news waiting for them once they arrived. The native helper who had worked with Richard in doing the Bible translation had a surprise. He along with some other Christian nationals had completed the translation of the Scripture from a copy they retained of Richard's work at Banmethuot after Richard and Lillian were captured and now they had a Bunong New Testament to present to them!! In addition, the hymnbook had been re-printed, as well! The Christians had hidden the precious translations in a hollow tree and the Viet Cong never found them! In time other translators finished the entire Old Testament, as well.

In 2011, Richard and Lillian returned to Vietnam for the centennial celebration of the work of the CMA in that country. The celebration was held in a sports stadium to accommodate the crowd of 12,000 Vietnamese and tribes people. The people swarmed to honor Richard and Lillian, to express their love for them, and to thank them for giving them the Word of God.

Richard spoke at the conference in the Bunong language to the crowd although it had been 36 years since he lived in the country. The ability to remember the language comes as no surprise to those of us who know Richard's unique mental capacity!

In 1975 there were 60,000 believers in Vietnam. Today there are 1.2 million. The graves of the martyrs are behind the pink house where Richard and Lillian lived.

"O for a thousand tongues to sing
My great Redeemer's praise

The glories of my God and King
The triumphs of His grace.

"My gracious Master and my God,
Assist me to proclaim
To spread through all the earth abroad
The honors of Thy name".
-Charles Wesley

CHAPTER 42
Richard's story

Richard was born on April 21, 1930 in Albany, Oregon. Both parents were 24 years old at the time. He is the only sibling to have been born in the United States. He left for China with his parents at age of 1 1/2 and did not return to live in the U.S until he was 13, except for a furlough visit when he was 8 years old.

He began school at Chefoo when he was 6 years old, the year that missionaries were evacuated from three northern interior provinces.

Mac and Lillian remained near Chefoo for 6 months as he adjusted to school. He later had one summer with them and saw them briefly at the time Kathy was enrolled in school. There were no visits after that. He lived away from his parents for most of 7 years with the exception of one furlough and he returned to the United States at age 13 years.

During his early school years Richard won the "Pendant" for the highest total track score at Chefoo when he was 10 years.

He was reunited with his parents and siblings in March of 1944 in Albany and he finished High School there. He won a prize for playing the baritone horn in a competition in Washington State.

He attended Wheaton College and earned a B.S. in Physics. At Wheaton he sang in the Men's Glee Club for three years where his beautiful voice would have had high value, and he played records for the campus radio station.

After graduation from Wheaton he attended Moody Bible Institute in Chicago and earned a diploma in Missions. He continued his studies at St. Paul Bible Institute, Summer Institute of Linguistics, Oregon State University and the University of Washington where he earned a M.A. in Linguistics.

In November of 1958, he sailed for Vietnam on a cargo ship after being appointed for missionary service by The Christian and Missionary Alliance. He was 28 years old.

Two years later he married Lillian, a missionary nurse already serving in Vietnam. They had 4 children, 2 girls and 2 boys.

After Richard and Lil were released from the Viet Cong in October of 1975, they remained in the US for two years while Richard completed his doctorate degree.

In 1977 Richard and Lil enrolled their four children at Ivory Coast Academy and then studied French in Paris. In November they arrived at their new station in Burkina Faso, West Africa where they served for 19 years. Richard, along with a team of helpers translated the NT and parts of the Old Testament in the Samo language.

Richard and Lillian retired after 38 years of missionary service with, The Christian and Missionary Alliance. They live in Oakdale, Minnesota.

Richard is a quiet, kind, brilliant servant-leader who is not only respected by everyone who knows him but also relied on for his uncanny memory for detail. Given an option of believing information listed in a dictionary and believing Richard, go with Richard! Avoid playing Scrabble with him unless you take loss well.

> "All the way my Savior leads me
> What have I to ask beside?
> Can I doubt His tender mercy?
> Who through life has been my Guide?
> Heavenly peace, divinest comfort,
> Here by faith in Him to dwell,
> For I know what ere befall me,
> Jesus doeth all things well."
> -Fanny Crosby

Epilogue

The Children of Missionaries (MK's)

In the summer of 1944, after many years in hiding, Anne Frank wrote in her diary, "I have lots of courage. I always feel so strong and as if I can bear a great deal. I feel so free and so young! I was glad when I first realized it, because I don't think I shall easily bow down before the blows that inevitably come to everyone."

Growing up as a child of missionaries brings opportunity to test the courage of many children. Being a missionary is not for the faint-hearted, but neither is being a missionary kid.

Sometimes missionary life is unfairly blamed for family problems it didn't generate. At other times it is viewed as pathology for which universal therapy is needed and from which one must recover. The experience of the missionary children in our family is told in this book not to condemn practices of the past related to the children of missionaries, but we cannot and should not rewrite history, although some of it is messy. Acknowledging the grief and loss does not invalidate the positive aspects of being an MK.

To presume that missionary life was harmful in the "olden days" when the events of this book occurred would be wrong. There was no automatic cause and effect. Some MK's did well in situations that were traumatic for others. Being a part of a missionary family did not guarantee a strong positive family. Geography seldom determines whether a home is healthy or unhealthy.

Mission practices now are not the same as at the time the stories in this book took place. Current psychological information has impacted selection, care and administration of personnel, changes in duration of service, the growing importance of member care world-wide, the changes in the social backgrounds of new missionaries, and all of this has had an impact on children.

Bryan Knell wrote that the word "missionary" has passed its "sell by date" and is now more unhelpful than helpful. Other dated language includes "pioneer missionary" and "mission compound," common language in our era. Without a doubt, missionary service today is very different than the time described in this book.

For some, being a MK was described as going into outer space, leaving home fast, coming down hard, and in between experiencing a totally different life. When the MK tried to share it, no one understood, or even wanted to understand.

MK's were often exposed to emotional, physical, or sexual abuse. In places where it was hard to be white, low-level emotional abuse such as touching, poking, crowding, laughing and teasing were like a constant background of radiation. People may not have understood that a child did not want to be closely surrounded by 40 on-lookers as he built a sand castle. Some of this happened to most MK's. Nationals may not have understood why they should not tease or tell lies, or threaten MK's with tales of demons or ghosts.

Older missionaries assumed resilience in MK's and their ability to cope. Mission Boards required that both mother and father were full-time missionaries and the care of children was relinquished to Amahs, other nationals, or to boarding schools. Many of these schools provided a better education than would have been received in the home country.

So, it is wrong to make generalizations about the impact of missions on children. What was traumatic for one child "built character" in another. Some children never shared painful incidents with their parents in an effort to protect their parents and their ministry, even at great harm to themselves. And, not all cultures were equally good.

Some stresses were unique to the decision of parents to be missionaries, such as support-raising furloughs in which children were expected to speak, sing and behave to make their parents look good. Being a missionary was sometimes considered the top echelon of Christianity. Missionaries were treated as special. Some parents developed a sense of entitlement in which they honestly believed their press releases and this impacted their ability to provide un-selfish nurture of their children. Children were left to meet the needs of their parents, not the other way around. Their children were more aware of the chinks in the armor of their parents than the budget committee of the home church.

Some stresses were no different than other children face in their home country, i.e. fathers who traveled and were gone from home weeks at a time, or separation from doting grandparents and extended family, for examples.

Re-entry to the home country was stressful for children who spent a part of their childhood overseas. Music, clothes, slang, and being an outsider to established friendships set them apart. MK's often had a superior education to peers in their home country and some tried to "dumb down" to avoid appearing intellectually superior. They had traveled extensively, often alone. They were different in so many ways, but desperate for friendship and acceptance.

The loss of an Amah had to be grieved and parents who felt threatened by the bond sometimes minimized the grief.

One study of missions conducted during the era of this book, found that approximately 25% of adult missionary kids looked back on their experience and described it as "the best childhood that could be imagined." The multiple advantages of cross-cultural life, the depth of spiritual experience, the early involvement in ministry had shaped their minds and hearts for extraordinary good. Another 55% of adult MK's state that growing up on the mission field brought equal amounts of pain and joy. And finally, 20% stated that being the child of missionaries wounded them in severe ways and left them with distorted views of God, the inability to establish and maintain intimate relationships, or left them with chronic depression or other life challenges.

One determinant of resilience in MK's is genetic inheritance. Children who were born to parents, who were neurologically sound, had high IQ's, physical and mental health, and children who had caregivers who were warm and nurturing were more likely to succeed.

We didn't all start out with equal does of qualities that make life easier. The more of these positive qualities available to a child the more likely it is that the mission field experience would be viewed as "wonderful."

In our own family Richard lived seven years separated from our parents as a young child. Kathy lived almost five years without them. Dave and Doris remained with our parents but lived with near constant and severe stress, nighttime escapes, and, irregular food. Chinese Christians frequently hid us while others were being killed. We all had un-treated serious illnesses, and were aware that our parents could die at any time and leave us as orphans.

At the same time, if you ask any of us we would all say that we developed a deep love for the Chinese people, grounding in Scripture, and a reliance on prayer.

We have all experienced healthy families of our own, enjoyed professional careers, and look back on our experience as missionary kids as enlarging and enriching our worlds. We are better people and our faith is more solid as a result of life on the mission field. We participated in a cause greater than ourselves.

The command to "Go into all the world and preach the Gospel" must be understood in the context of Matthew 18: "If you cause one of these little (missionary) children to stumble, it would be better if a millstone were tied around your neck and you were cast into the sea." There is not greater apologetic for the care of missionary children than the fact that God said to do it.

It is true, "The blood of the martyrs is the seed of the church", but some of that blood was spilled on children of missionaries. It is and was costly business to follow Christ.

> "Thou hast given me the heritage of those that fear thy name."
> Psalm 61:5 TLB

Dr. Doris Sanford

About the author…

Dr. Doris Sanford has spoken internationally on issues related to the emotional care of children, as well as being interviewed on national TV programs in several countries.

Dr. Sanford is the author of 30 books for or about children and multiple magazine articles including, Decision Magazine and, The Association of Christian Schools International. She served as the trainer for directors of Royal Family Kids Camps, which provides camps for abused children and is on the Board of Directors for, Music for the Soul, a record company providing music for hurting adults and children.

Doris maintained a private practice as a Consultant for the State of Oregon, Foster Care Division until her retirement. She currently is busy with four awesome grandchildren.

For more information on the Phillips family story or to contact Doris Sanford, please email doris.e.sanford@gmail.com

1944469R00122

Made in the USA
San Bernardino, CA
21 February 2013